The Happy Mommy Handbook:
The Ultimate How-to Guide on Keeping Your Toddlers and Preschoolers Busy, Out of Trouble and Motivated to Learn

Katie Norris
and
Susan Case

AWOC.COM Publishing
Denton, Texas

AWOC.COM Publishing
P.O. Box 2819
Denton, TX 76202

Manufactured in the United States of America

ISBN: 978-1-62016-010-7

Katie's blog: mommywithselectivememory.com
Susan's blog: kindergartenbasics.blogspot.com

A Special Note of Thanks

Thank you to the following people for their photo contributions: Lisa Beedle, Kim Moore, Mark Dulin, Rachael Linton and Katie Norris. We would also like to thank the following blogs for their photos: Teach Preschool, Mom to 2 Posh Lil Divas, The Golden Gleam, Nurture Store, Little Stories, and In Leiu of Preschool. And a special thank you to Get Moore Designs for the cover.

Dedication

I would like to thank our wonderful editor, Katie Ernzen, who spent her free time editing the book. I cannot thank her enough for her contribution. Thank you to my parents for believing in me and spending so many years editing my papers before I really knew how to write. You inspire me daily to be the best parent I can be. Thank you to my best friend Dani for all your support. Thank you to Sara for taking the time to read the rough draft and encouraging me. Thank you to my darling husband for tolerating my writing hobby and listening to me when frustrated. Thank you to Susan Case. Your friendship has truly been a wonderful addition to my life and I am honored to have the opportunity to write this book with you. Most of all, thank you to my incredible kids. You are the light of my life and this entire book was written because playing with you is so much fun. ~ Katie Norris

This book is dedicated to my four siblings. My sister Diane Atkinson once again helped me edit a book and encouraged me throughout the process. My other siblings, John, Mark and Shryl are always supportive. I'm grateful we can laugh our way through the memories of growing up together and reminisce about the countless hours of playing outside. This book would not have been possible without my husband Dan's help and encouragement and my daughter Sarah's journey with me through the educational experiences. But the idea, inspiration, perseverance, and enthusiasm are entirely due to Katie Norris, who is always looking for ways to teach her children through play. ~ Susan Case

Table of Contents

Introduction
Why Real Moms Need Real Help

Charlotte Brown saved up for seven months to buy herself an iPad. She fell in love the moment she downloaded her first App. She could not stop telling everyone about it. However, the infatuation soon began to wear off as her two-year-old also discovered the wonders of the iPad. Charlotte was peacefully scrolling through the news one morning when Eva ran over and said, "Mommy, *my* iPad."

Charlotte tried to resist giving Eva the iPad. She knew that experts said little kids should have limited screen time, but as a stay-at-home mom, there always came a time in the day when she needed a few minutes to do the dishes or fold laundry in peace.

Why couldn't Eva just play with her own toys? She had an entire room full of expensive toys. Why wasn't that enough?

One morning Charlotte needed to pay some bills. She tried to get her daughter interested in playing with blocks, but Eva kept begging for the iPad. By now, Eva knew how to turn it on and even find her favorite Apps. Charlotte half-heartedly protested for a few minutes, but finally gave in. She was working quietly for a few minutes when she heard a crash. She hopped out of her chair and turned around, only to see her precious iPad lying on the floor, shattered.

Eva huddled next to it with a worried look on her face. She looked at her mom and said, "Mommy, new iPad?"

At this point, Charlotte realized that something in her life had to change. After she got over the heartbreak of losing her expensive iPad, she consulted her best friend and fellow mom and explained the situation. Charlotte's friend, Katie Norris, explained to Charlotte that she needed to challenge Eva, to provide her with stimulating and educational activities. She suggested that Charlotte buy a bag of large buttons from Hobby Lobby.

Charlotte was hesitant. She didn't want extra stuff to clean up. She wanted to simplify her life, not complicate it. Plus, how could Eva really benefit from playing with buttons? Katie explained to Charlotte that the process of pouring is very important for young children. They learn coordination and practice fine motor skills *and* it's challenging so it captures their attention.

Charlotte had no idea that pouring was important. In fact, when Eva tried to pour her own drinks, Charlotte intercepted so she didn't make a big mess. She was still skeptical, but the next day when it was time to clean up the morning dishes, she did as her friend suggested and put Eva at the kitchen table with several different cups, a muffin tin, and a bowl of buttons large enough so that they weren't a choking hazard. The buttons she found were different colors and shapes. Charlotte poured them into a cup with some hesitation—how much fun could Eva really have with a bunch of buttons? However, she became amazed. Charlotte sat with Eva for the first couple of minutes and showed her how to pour the buttons back and forth. She showed her how the buttons could be organized by color. Charlotte praised Eva when she was able to pour the buttons from cup to cup. When Charlotte got up to do the dishes several minutes later, she held her breath to see what would happen. Eva didn't hop down and demand the iPad. Instead, she played for 20 more minutes with those simple buttons. She poured them back and forth, and back and forth.

Then she started putting them in the different muffin tins, sorting them by color.

Then something else amazing happened. Eva got down from the table and suddenly was able to play independently with her own toys. It was like Charlotte had a new kid! She was able to finish the dishes, put dinner in the crock-pot, *and* check her email! Not only that, Charlotte realized that for the first time in days she didn't feel frustrated or guilty about how Eva was spending her free time. Instead, she was able to watch her daughter, and interact with her, while she actually learned something.

We probably all know moms like Charlotte, moms who want to be present in their kids' lives and spend quality time, but the reality is, moms have a lot to do. Experts say we should limit the time our kids watch television, but we have to wonder whether these "experts" understand how hard it is just to keep up with the laundry, the bills, and the dishes.

On top of all the chores we moms must do around the house, we are also the main educators for our young children. Only 25 percent of the human brain is developed at birth. Parents cannot just wait until they enter school to educate them. Why? Because brain development occurring *before* the age of five lays the foundation for future intellect; these are the most important years of a child's development. Yet how can a busy Mom find the time to stimulate her young child's brain when there are other siblings to take care of and chores to do around the house? That is what we intend to show you with this book.

Children have lots of needs. They need love, food, shelter, and clothing. They also need short bursts of "Mommy and Me" time. That time can be reading a book, dancing, or even just talking. Give them your focused attention for an uninterrupted 15 minutes then enjoy amazing results. Sometimes it can be sensory integration through experimenting with different textures and medians, such as playdough or paint. Sometimes it can be fine motor activities, such as stringing beads or pouring sand. Sometimes it is as simple as using a plain piece of paper and crayons to express themselves. Look at their masterpiece. Ask them to tell you what they did and look in their eyes as they express their thoughts to you. Then communicate with them as if they are the most important people on earth; after all, that is how they view you.

Once you have invested this quality time, children tend to feel content again and are able to use their imagination to invent their own games. This means that mom *and* dad suddenly have some free time to finish their tasks while watching their child from a distance.

Giving moms free time can be a wonderful gift to the whole family. Recently published research has explored the topic of whether a mother's level of frustration can affect a child in their long-term development. A study published in the *Proceedings from the National Academy of Sciences* titled "Maternal Support in Early Childhood Predicts Larger Hippocampal Volumes at School Age" supports the fact that moms influence their child's brain development. They studied a group of children over several years and found that a child whose mother is harsh and scolding has a smaller brain mass by 10 percent than a child whose mother is nurturing and helpful. Of course, many other factors influence brain mass and intelligence, such as genetics, sleep, and the environment, but this study gives further evidence that we need to find ways to help mothers have more patience when kids are fighting and whining. Moms can only take so much; we are only human!

So how can a mom be more nurturing and avoid being frustrated with her children? Moms tend to be frustrated when kids are acting badly. Therefore, if kids act better, life will be more fun and mom will able to have more patience. A child who is offered interesting and challenging activities has fewer behavior problems. Period. We can't expect children to be well behaved all the time, but the more opportunities children have for play, exploration and discovery, the smarter they will be *and* the better they will behave.

Windows of opportunity are sensitive periods in children's lives when specific types of learning take place. Early stimulation sets the stage for how children will learn and interact with others throughout their lifetime. A child's experiences, good or bad, influence the wiring of his brain and the connections in his nervous system.

Babies are born ready to learn with a natural curiosity and playfulness. They are motivated to make sense of their world as explorers and pattern-seekers. Trillions of connections between brain cells are being made before a child enters Kindergarten. Children need solid relationships and hands-on fun experiences to reach their full potential. You, their lifeline and greatest source of comfort and love, are also their greatest resource to help them engage in activities that match their individual skills, needs and interests. The wonderful part is that children naturally want activities that are developmentally appropriate, challenging and rewarding.

Research shows that brain development does not stop after early childhood, but it is the *foundation* upon which the brain continues developing. Early childhood is the time to build either a strong and supportive foundation, or a fragile and unreliable one. These early years are very important in the development that continues in childhood, adolescence and adulthood.

It is well documented that children in our society are experiencing alarming increases in obesity, health disorders, and screen time with noticeably less playtime. Children pushed into academics too soon may miss out on a more integrative, curiosity-driven approach to learning that they will need later in life. In our society, parents often feel pressure that even at a young age children should be "ahead of the curve" in terms of learning letters, math, and how to read. However, young children do not care about "getting ahead" of others; they are interested in exploring and discovering in their own way and feeling safe, connected, and loved. Parents are sometimes surprised and disappointed when their young child is not interested in flashcards. But the fact is that routine unconnected learning of numbers, letters and phonetic sounds is not that exciting for children. Instead, children enjoy learning through relevant, hands-on, safe, positive, fun play, which builds their confidence and self-esteem, resulting in fewer behavior problems.

This book focuses on learning through play, the way children are naturally wired to develop. It is written from two voices: a mom and a teacher. Katie Norris has two small children and writes a successful "Mommy" blog geared toward other moms. She is a real mom who makes real mistakes and is not afraid to admit them. But she has also spent countless hours researching ways to stimulate her children and has been amazed at the amount of free time this has given her. Children learn to find things to do and use their imaginations when they are intellectually stimulated and given opportunities to discover through play.

Susan Case also writes a successful blog and is the author of *Kindergarten: Tattle-Tales, Tools, Tactics, Triumphs, and Tasty Treats for Teachers and Parents.* She is a retired Kindergarten, special education, and early childhood teacher with a Masters in Family and Child Development. Susan and Katie began collaborating on various subjects on their blogs including sensory and fine motor development and the importance of learning through play. The reaction to their collaborations continues to be very positive from moms and teachers in need of advice and resources.

After Katie's friend Charlotte experienced the iPad meltdown, Katie realized that there are a lot of moms who could benefit from a little direction in finding stimulating projects for young children. Thus, *The Happy Mommy Handbook* was born.

The driving force behind this book is the desire to help moms create an environment where children can learn from playful, developmentally appropriate activities, some guided and directed by a parent, but many self-initiated. Flexible and extended activities are also included as well as step-by-step instructions and a shopping list of basic supplies. (See Chapter Three.) These activities take into account the age, experience, interests and abilities of young children and will foster a child's in-born motivation and inquisitiveness, giving you the reassurance that you are providing opportunities for growth in all the areas of development. Your children will be healthier, happier and smarter, experiencing fewer problems with stress, anxiety, depression, obesity, and behavior.

The goals of writing this book are simple: (1) to give you more free time while growing smarter and happier children, and (2) to encourage you to enjoy and make the most of these early years because they are extremely important and will fly by quickly.

In everything you do in your family, keep in mind the miracle of the Chinese bamboo tree. After the seed for this amazing tree is planted, you see nothing, absolutely nothing, for four years except for a tiny shoot coming out of a bulb. During those four years, all the growth is underground in a massive, fibrous root structure that spreads deep and wide in the earth. But then in the fifth year the Chinese bamboo tree grows up to eighty feet! Many things in family life are like the Chinese bamboo tree. You work and you invest time and effort, and you do everything you can possibly do to nurture growth, and sometimes you don't see anything for weeks, months, or even years. But if you're patient and keep working and nurturing, that "fifth year" will come, and you will be astonished at the growth and change you see taking place. ~ Stephen R. Covey

Part I
The Early Years

Chapter One
Keeping Kids Busy with Sensory Activities

Mommy's Dilemma

One night when my daughter was a little over two years old, I was trying to cook dinner. I was overly ambitious that night, wanting to impress my husband with some delicious stir-fry. That sounds easy enough, but it takes a very sharp knife to cut broccoli, and it's not exactly safe to hold your kid on your hip while you cook stir-fry. I reached for the remote, but really didn't want to turn on the television. I also had a baby at the time, so my daughter was already watching way too many television shows and DVDs throughout the day while I tried to feed a fussy baby.

Instead, I decided to try an experiment my friend had recommended. I got out my Tupperware container full of sand, some funnels and cups, and I situated my daughter at the kitchen table. I showed her what to do with the sand. Then I watched in amazement while she played with the sand for an entire 40 minutes! She was mesmerized by it. She kept pouring it back and forth into the cups over and over and over again. Not only did I finish my stir-fry before my husband walked in the door from a very busy day, but I also sat with her when I was finished with dinner and paid all the bills. I sighed with contentment. There was hope for us.

Teacher's Advice

The beauty of this scenario is that the mom, Katie Norris, was rewarded with some free time, *and* her daughter also benefitted. Lucy learned during the time she played with sand. While Lucy poured sand back and forth, she learned about gravity and she enhanced her fine motor skills. Children learn by doing things that are interesting and relevant to them—or just for pure sensory/integration fun. Even young children can spend 20 or 30 minutes on an activity that is age appropriate and challenging. Opportunity, praise, and encouragement will help your child develop skills. Think about that for a second. You have a chance to cook dinner in peace while the kids are actually learning and benefitting from independent time. The sand experiment was just scratching the surface. There is a whole world that can be opened up to your child involving fine motor skills and sensory play.

What is Sensory Integration?

Sensory integration is the ability to take in information through the senses of touch, movement, smell, taste, vision and hearing, and to combine the resulting perceptions with prior information, memories and knowledge already stored in the brain. In other words, children learn by exploring and discovering using their five senses and movement. Young children are eager learners, but due to their limited language they learn more from hands-on experiences. Of course, we know they explore by putting things into their mouth. But they also love feeling interesting textures, smelling different scents, hearing rhythmic/rhyming music and words, seeing/observing everything around them, and moving/interacting in their fascinating world.

More and more children are being diagnosed with having sensory/integration issues. In other words, their bodies have problems encoding sensory stimulation. Therapies involve swinging, sliding, and rolling on large plastic balls just to name a few techniques. If you feel that your child needs a professional evaluation, it is best to seek an evaluation early because the earlier the intervention, the greater the success. Ask your child's pediatrician about developmental milestones or call your public school district and express your concerns. Free evaluations are offered starting at birth as is mandated by federal law. If a diagnoses is determined that your child has sensory/integration or even expressive delays, therapies are available and free. Some communities even offer free therapeutic horseback riding lessons to children with special needs. There is ample research to document that animals can help children's development and happiness by teaching them responsibility, learning to follow sequenced instructions, gaining physical exercise or just because animals are not judgmental and they love unconditionally.

The Five Senses

Encourage your child to be still and **hear** different sounds such as the wind, soft music, bells, humming, laughing, sneezing, whistling, ice cubes melting, ocean waves, a rock thrown in water, rain, eating an apple, crying, breathing, birds chirping and anything else imaginable.

Children love to **feel** objects such as using playdough and finger paint. If you want your child to enjoy books, start with ones that have interesting things to touch, pull, push (sound buttons), pop-up or manipulate in some manner.

Children enjoy the sense of **smell**. Put different scents into baggies or jars and enjoy watching them experience scents and odors. They could smell vanilla extract, perfumes, flowers, onions, lavender, vinegar (pickles) and scented oils. Put scents in playdough for extra enjoyment.

Let children **taste** different items that are salty (pretzels), sour (lemons, pickles), sweet (candy) and bitter (olives).

Your child will love to **see** what happens when they mix paint, melt colored ice cubes (food coloring), play with shaving cream, or use chalk, crayons and markers.

Movement is not considered one of the five senses but it is an important part of sensory integration. Children explore and feel through their body's movements, gravity, and spatial awareness.

How to Do Sensory Activities at Home

Now it's time for some fun! While you set up these activities for your child, it's important to stay involved. These are designed to give you free time, but children need guidance from parents in order to learn. Eventually, they will understand what to do with the materials and the boundaries for using them.

Sensory Box

Use a small shallow cardboard box or even a large bowl to fill with different kinds of objects. Offer choices of pasta, beads, dried beans, buttons, puff balls, spoons, or anything you have handy that a child will enjoy. For a bit messier experience, layer the bottom with rice, sand, sugar, beans or popcorn. Encourage them to place favorite objects in the box such as action figures, cars or Legos and use their imaginations for extended playtime. Give them different kinds of cups and spoons for pouring and making sounds. Offer an empty toilet paper or paper towel roll so they can slide things into the box, using it like a ramp or a tunnel. Children love rolling marbles through the rolls but must be closely supervised with small objects that could cause a choking hazard. Long gift wrapping rolls offer hours of

* indoors: cotton ball bin c spoons, tp roll
* outdoors: sand or rice bin c cars, spoons, tp roll, gift wrap roll

fun of rolling objects through the tube while standing. Extending this would be to tape together tubes going in different directions creating a maze for marble play.

With encouragement and praise, your child will want to sort the objects helping you clean up and organize them again. Model the process by sorting same objects into the designated containers. Their participation will teach them responsibility, respect for materials, and recycling concepts.

⁷ Playdough

Playdough offers an amazing array of opportunities for learning and fun. This is a relatively clean activity and easy to clean up, as long as you only offer a few colors at a time and use on an easy-to-clean surface. You can buy kits with good playdough toys such as rolling pins, mini muffin tins, very small cookie sheets, garlic crusher and potato masher. Small children often like to tear playdough into small pieces but this is normal and can be balled up afterward with minimal problems. Children enjoy plastic cookie cutters shaped like hearts, trains, flowers, dinosaurs, or holiday themes which can be purchased after the holidays on sale.

Show them how to manipulate and use their hands to make things happen. Roll a long, thin piece, then model how to cut it up into little pieces using child safety scissors or a plastic knife. Playdough is one of the most malleable and inexpensive materials made for children offering them endless possibilities for creativity. It isn't messy if supervised and used on an old plastic tablecloth or trash bag.

Playdough Provides Many Benefits Including:

- Fine Motor by strengthening fingers, hands and wrists,
- Cognitive by offering opportunities to teach letters, colors, shapes, and counting,
- Imaginative Play by placing different objects into the dough such as buttons, sprinkles, beads or action figures,
- Self-Esteem by giving children the opportunity to create whatever they want gaining some mastery and control over their environment,
- De-stressor offering a safe release for tension or angry feelings by squeezing, twisting, punching, poking, throwing on a mat or designated area, and
- Mom Rewarding because after initial boundaries are set, mommy may have some "down-time."

Cooked Playdough

2 cups flour
4 tsp cream of tartar
1 cup salt
2 tbsp cooking oil
2 cups water
food coloring and scent (optional)

Mix dry ingredients together in old pan on top of the stove. Add oil, food coloring and hot water. Cook on low mixing ingredients together until right consistency. Drop on wax paper and as soon as cool enough knead until smooth. If playdough is too dry, add more water, a little at a time. If playdough is too crumbly, knead in a small amount of oil. Store in an airtight container.

No-Cook Playdough
2 cups self-rising flour
2 tbsp alum (in spice section)
2 tbsp salt
2 tbsp cooking oil
1 and ¼ boiling cup water
Food coloring and scent (optional)

Mix oil and food coloring together before adding to dry mixture. Mix ingredients until pliable. Keep in a container or sealed plastic bag when not in use.

Sand

Fine sand is available from hobby and toy stores, your local pet store, and some hardware stores. More coarse sand is available in the gardening centers at major retailers. You'll need a rectangular plastic container with a tight fitting lid that is about 8" x 11" and very shallow. Fill it halfway with sand and keep the lid for storage. Then give your child a few pouring toys, such as a funnel, small tablespoon from the kitchen, and a small plastic cup. Again, step back and watch the magic. When they are finished, store the Tupperware® in a closet with the lid secure. Other objects to play with in fine sand are colanders and sturdy gift-wrapping rolls. Sand sounds scary but it's really not, especially if you spend adequate time discussing boundaries and rules before they are allowed to use the sand. You might have to vacuum a small mess, but as long as they don't get wild and start throwing sand, the mess won't be too bad. If they do act wild and crazy, take it away. They will beg you to give it back and will be more careful the next time.

Water

Kids *love* water. For long periods of enjoyment, give them a big plastic mixing bowl or bucket full of water with various pouring options, such as small cups, big cups, measuring cups, spoons, floatable and sinkable objects, and plastic teapots. Ask them to be careful trying to keep as much water as possible in the container and give them a small hand towel. Ask them to clean up messes as they go. You can offer small margarine tubs with holes cut in the bottom. When they pour water they can watch it come out the bottom. Young children are fascinated with gravity and velocity for long periods of time.

You could also get a small stool so they can reach the sink. Turn on the faucet very low and give them a few cups. This is really fun, but a waste of water so you might want to limit the time on this activity. Children must always be supervised when near water. If your child is playing in the bathtub or sink, they *must* be supervised.

> **Tip:** To prevent accidental burns from hot water, turn down the temperature at your hot water source. You do not need scalding water coming out of your faucet!

An extended water activity is hours of fun with water beads which come in beautiful colors and expand when wet. Let your child play with them awhile before being near water such as sorting or rolling activities or dropping them through tubes. Water beads are available at crafts and toy stores, some dollar stores, or on-line stores like Amazon (http://amzn.to/I3Egf7).

Painting

Children love to see, mix, and paint with bright colors. Buy washable paints and let them paint! It can be messy, and must be supervised, but your child will love you for letting them paint. They can use a cotton swab with white paint on black paper, blow paint through a straw (teach blowing with water first so they don't suck paint), or even paint outside just using water from a bucket and a brush. Mix a little glue with paint and let children stick objects on paper or on a box or mix some water-soluble paint with dish soap and they can help you clean windows. Hobby stores have window paint which is washable from glass so children can enjoy producing art before helping you wash windows.

If you are worried about painting indoors, try purchasing a small tub of washable paint. Save the container and then you can re-use it each time. This contains the paint and the mess.

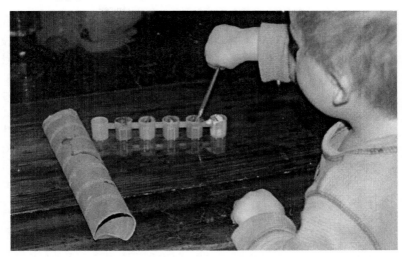

Painting is also a great way to make personalized gifts for people. You can buy wooden figurines and ceramic ornaments at your favorite hobby store and your children can take great pride in their finished product. Use a permanent marker to put the child's name and date on the back of gifts.

Shaving cream on cookie sheet

This is a fun, easy-to-clean way to do finger painting. Just put shaving cream on a cookie sheet and show them how to move it around with their hands. You could give them a paintbrush or cotton swab to explore the foam. Keep an eye on them so they don't get this in their eyes. Add a dab of food coloring or scent for extra sensory investigation. Shaving cream will take away crayon marks and germs from surfaces such as their work/play table. Your child will be proud to have helped you clean!

Books

Children love books with interesting things to touch and explore such as material books, pop-up books for manipulation, sticker books, or books about animals with different textures. Keep books available when you need some down time. We have dedicated a chapter to help in the development of reading skills (See Chapter Nine.)

Tip: Moms you do not have to do this type of activity all day long or every day. If your child is playing happily, do not interrupt him. Your child will let you know when he is ready for some "Mommy and Me" time by acting whiny and needy. At that point, introduce one of these fun activities or just read them a book.

To know is nothing at all; to imagine is everything.
~ Albert Einstein

Chapter Two
Keeping Kids Busy With Fine Motor Activities

Mommy's Dilemma

When my daughter was about three and a half years old, our local elementary school invited us to a "fun" program for children ages three to five. The idea was to offer crafts and games and to give parents an opportunity to meet the local Kindergarten teacher. I was really excited and so was my daughter.

We found a little table right away and my daughter happily started coloring. Eventually, the Kindergarten teacher walked over to us. She seemed very warm and we introduced ourselves.

"This is my daughter," I said. "She's three and is very excited to be here."

The teacher looked down at Lucy and smiled, but then grabbed the crayon right out of her hand!

"She's coloring the wrong way. See? She's making a fist," the teacher said. "You really need to break that habit before she gets to Kindergarten. You wouldn't believe how many children come to Kindergarten and are still coloring this way! It's because they don't have strong enough muscles. You really need to work on fine motor skills and fast! Here, honey, do it like this," she continued to my horror. She grabbed Lucy's hand and pressed her fingers together and contorted the crayon so Lucy was coloring with her fingers "pinching" the crayon.

The teacher walked away and everyone was staring at us. It had never entered my mind before to think about how she was holding her crayon. This wasn't exactly turning out to be the fun experience I had in mind. I began to panic. *She needs therapy! She's going to need extra help! If I was a good mommy, she would already be holding her pencil correctly! Maybe if I didn't work, I would be able to cultivate her fine motor skills...* My self-berating went ON and ON and ON— general frantic thoughts of a doting mommy.

Teacher's Advice

The good news is that Lucy was *only* three. There is still plenty of time to nurture her fine motor skills so that she can learn how to hold a pencil correctly. Building her self-esteem and playing/learning with developmentally appropriate activities are far more important than doing something she is not ready to do.

Using Developmentally Appropriate Practices means meeting learners where they are—not necessarily where they should be—and taking into consideration the growth areas of the whole child including physical, emotional, social, and cognitive levels. It means providing learning opportunities that are challenging, yet achievable. In other words, it means teaching with consideration to age, experience, interests, and abilities of an individual child. Children learn by taking "baby steps." But they do need to be challenged and given educational opportunities so that they may reach their highest potential.

The ability to correctly grasp a pencil is achieved after the large and small muscles have gone through stages. There is a process of development called "big to small" or "proximal to distal." This means that children develop the larger muscles of the trunk, shoulders and arms before the smaller muscles of the hands, wrists and fingers. Using the finger muscles to correctly grasp a pencil can only be accomplished when the muscles are strong enough and the child is interested and willing.

Fine motor skill is the ability to use fingers, hands and arms together to reach, grasp and manipulate small objects and use tools like forks, spoons, crayons, and scissors. It is the coordination of small muscle movements, especially the fingers with vision, to accomplish a task and prepare a child to eat with utensils, turn pages in a book, turn knobs, pinch objects, transfer objects from one hand to another, use writing tools, manipulate keyboards, and dress themselves. It is quite an accomplishment when a child is able to tie shoes, button, and zip so praise lavishly in their attempts.

Developing fine motor skills can be frustrating and challenging for some children. Watch your child's level of frustration. Gradually increase the time of activities. This play/work time needs to be pleasurable, attainable, and rewarding so that your child will continue to engage and make progress.

Help Increase Fine Motor Skills

Make materials available so your child can:

- **Push** objects through a slot like pennies or buttons into a Piggy Bank or container with a slit in the lid, or push pegs into a board like golf tees into Styrofoam or Fuzzy Sticks into a colander.
- **Pick up** marbles and put them in a jar. For variety, have child stand up and drop marbles into a bucket or drop balls or other small objects into containers, boxes or sacks.
- **Build** with blocks, Lincoln Logs, Legos, and egg cartons.
- **Lace** with lacing cards—poke string through holes and pull.
- **Grasp** wooden puzzles pieces and place correctly.
- **Arrange** rocks, leaves, beans, cards, pasta, sticks or whatever interests child.

- **Manipulate** playdough and clay. Pull, press, stretch, roll, pound, squeeze, twist, pinch.
- **Squeeze** glue bottles, water guns, and sponges.
- **Shake** bottles of glitter or baking sprinkles.
- **Bead** necklaces with yarn or pasta wheels with lacing string.
- **Mark** with fat pencils, crayons, markers, and sidewalk chalk.
- **Pour** sand, water, salt, sugar, rice, or beans using bowls, funnels, spoons, cups, tubes, cardboard wrapping rolls, and colanders.
- **Sort** small objects with interesting textures like cotton balls, pom-poms, pastas, sponges, and rocks placing them into egg cartons or empty yogurt containers.

Specific Fine Motor Activities

Pennies in a slot jar

A perfect material for this is an empty salt container. Take out the silver piece on the top and discard. Fill a small bowl with pennies and guide your child to fill the salt container with pennies or game tokens. Even toddlers enjoy this activity and it can be emptied again and again. Vary this exercise using different containers and objects. Children enjoy ownership so it would be fun for them to decorate and have their name on their personal fine motor container. You could even decorate your own to add to the fun.

> Note to Moms: Don't let these activities overwhelm you or stress you out. These are intended to be used if you need something to do with your children. However, if your kids are happily playing on their own, don't interrupt and demand that they string a bead necklace. Important self-learning skills are being developed while they are entertaining themselves in productive play.

Beading Necklaces

Several pieces of old shoelaces can be used if you don't have lacing string. Tie a good knot at the bottom and provide material for stringing. You can buy beads or use pasta such as pinwheel or rigatoni (tubular). This activity is really fun for them because they can wear the necklace afterward or even have their dolls or action figures wear it. Then you can take off the beads and do it again later. Did you know that there are over 500 different kinds of pasta? The exploration possibilities are enormous. Children can even practice making a necklace in a special pattern. Show them how pretty it looks when you lace one blue, then one red, then one blue, and so on to continue a simple pattern to more complex patterns when they are ready. This will help develop math and reading skills also.

Recipe for Colorful Pasta or Rice

In a zip bag, put ¼ cup rubbing alcohol (or use vinegar) and at least 10 drops of food coloring and swish it around. Then, add 1 to 2 cups of pinwheel pasta. Turn bag over occasionally. The longer the pasta sits—the brighter the colors. Dry on wax paper, or newspaper, on cookie sheets. Children will love making different colors by mixing food color drops.

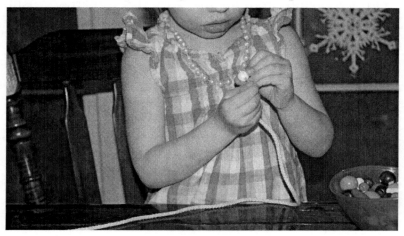

Stickers

Kids find stickers irresistible. Sometimes people see them as just a waste of money, but do not be fooled. Children have to use a lot of concentration to peel the stickers and then they can use their creativity to design something special. Stickers can be found in almost any subject that interests your child, such as princesses, cars, animals, monsters, sea creatures, or relating to holidays or events. Think of a

good background color and tape construction paper in a convenient place for them such as a sliding glass door or a wall using masking tape, which removes easily.

Push Pin Activity

A standard pin cushion, normally used for sewing, and some long push pins with a large head will be needed for this activity. You will also need a Parmesan shaker or a strainer.

Model pushing pins into the holes. During activities, explain what you are doing to help your child learn new vocabulary.

Tracing and Cutting

This activity takes a lot of concentration and is probably not ideal until children are at least three. Draw any shape on a piece of paper. Then give your child a jumbo-sized push pin and show them how to poke holes in the tracing. If they poke enough holes in it, you can eventually cut it out for them, using only the holes they made. It probably takes a hundred pokes, so it's a great activity for enhancing concentration and fine motor skills. The beauty is that you can make any shape you like such as hearts, their favorite cartoon character, letters to spell their name, an action figure hero, fish, animals or whatever interests your child.

Tongs and Spoons

For this project, use small tongs that are not sharp, plastic tweezers, or a large spoon. Put small objects in a bowl on the left such as pom-poms, cotton balls or large beads. Place an empty bowl on the right and encourage your child to transfer the objects from the left to the right using the tongs, tweezers or spoon. This begins the process of crossover of mid-section or moving hand and arm from left to right, which will help develop writing and even reading skills.

Sorting

You can buy a sorting game, such as colored bears, or you can create your own using buttons, beads, rocks, colored dominoes, or pom-poms. Have several colors of bowls and show them how to sort each color into the correct bowl. You could also use a muffin tin or egg carton and encourage them to sort into the different compartments. Model how to sort by putting several same-type objects into the containers and repeating the descriptive words, "Put all the red ones in here, the blue ones in here, and yellow in here." Or "Put the circles here, squares here, and triangles here." You can cut shapes out of felt or colored paper. Material or cardstock will survive longer.

Squeeze bottle Skills

Start with 2/3 cups each of salt, flour, and water. Let your child pour ingredients into a bowl and mix thoroughly with a whisk. The liquid will be fairly thick. Pour the mixture into four different squeeze bottles and then let your children choose colors to add of your Tempra paint. Squeeze some to the top of each bottle. Protect your table and let the fun begin. Let them squeeze all the colors onto paper or even old scraps of cardboard so you can keep the results. This is great for building strength. You could even lightly spell out names with glue and encourage them to trace over the letters by squeezing the paint.

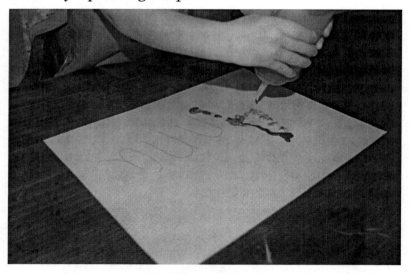

Another way to build fine motor skills is to fill a medicine dropper with water and squeeze onto paper or cardboard, or even a file folder. This would be much more interesting if the water was colored with a few drops of food coloring. The primary colors are red, blue and yellow. Three bowls with these colors would allow the child to mix the colors on the paper resulting in many different colors. It doesn't take much money to entertain a young child. Everything is amazing to them as they discover, manipulate, and enlarge their world.

Pouring

Pouring is a very versatile activity. Starting at about age 18 months, most kids can pour. You can offer colored rice, buttons, beads, popcorn, sugar, water, pasta or perhaps old cornmeal (depending on your nerves and their obedience to play with it over the container). However, the trick is only offering one thing at a time. Sit them at the kitchen table and give them two or three pouring options, such as a plastic liquid measuring cup, a small disposable party cup, and a ½ cup measuring cup. You could even buy paper party cups and print letters on them for letter recognition, like Ss for sugar. Offer one type of material, such as colored rice and fill the measuring cup half full with the material. Then walk away and watch the magic. Change materials when they grow tired of the original, but it's important to put away the first one before moving on so that it will stay fresh and special.

Scissors

Children love cutting things with scissors—changing the shape and forming something different. It gives them a sense of control, power, and independence. Have your child roll playdough or pizza dough into snakes and show them how to cut. Scissor cutting should be supervised. It may be easier for them to hold foam to cut before progressing to old magazines and newspaper. They will love to making a collage out of favorite clippings from magazines.

Tape

Children can entertain themselves for hours with masking tape. Like scissors, it is intriguing for them to play with because parents are hesitant to give their children tape. Your children see you use it and are curious and want to be like you. They may not be able to tear masking tape yet, but you could tape long pieces hanging from a table and see what happens. Maybe they'd like to stick that outdated pasta on the tape.

Caution: Always keep an eye on children, even when they seem to be working well on something. One mom told me she was busy on the phone and when she re-entered the living room, she found maxi-pads taped all around the coffee table. Little Caroline was beaming and proud of her accomplishment. You never know what kind of mischief they can get into when your back is turned.

Bubble Wrap

Need some down time? Can your child pop bubble-wrap? If not with their fingers, they will love stomping on it, giving you a little relief and space.

Somehow I can't believe that there are any heights that can't be scaled by a man who knows the secrets of making dreams come true. This special secret, it seems to me, can be summarized in four Cs. They are curiosity, confidence, courage, and constancy, and the greatest of all is confidence. ~ Walt Disney

Chapter Three
Crafts and Art Projects

Mommy's Dilemma

I used to hate rainy days. Being stuck in the house all day with two little kids was not my idea of a good time. The day always started off fine. We would eat breakfast, then the kids got down and played and things were all right for about fifteen minutes. Then it was as if my kids got an email that said, "Your job today is to irritate your sibling." This strongly worded memo seemed to outline specifics, "Do everything you can to irritate people. If your brother wants a toy, steal it from him. If he is playing happily with something, go sit on his toy and break it, then demand to know why he's crying."

At that point, I would half-heartedly consider going somewhere, but dragging two kids, a diaper bag, and an umbrella while my feet splashed through puddles was not very appealing either.

I eventually just turned on the TV for the kids when it rained and always felt guilty about it. Then, one day we went to a friend's house and she pulled out some toilet paper rolls and craft paper. My daughter's eyes lit up and she was immediately intrigued. My friend showed the girls how to glue the paper together. Then she pulled out some googly eyes.

Lucy was in heaven. She and her friend giggled while they glued on eyes and a nose then drew on a mouth. Lucy was so proud of her little creation that she talked about it for the next three days. At that point, I knew that I needed to overcome my fear of crafting and figure this whole thing out. My friend and her daughter seemed to really be *enjoying* each other. Then it hit me: Life with kids *should* be fun. Rainy days don't have to be excruciating. We as parents *should* spend a large portion of our day laughing with our kids and watching as they explore the world. Maybe working on crafts was a way to do that, especially on rainy days.

However, I was forced to admit that there are two types of moms out there:

1. Moms who love to craft and are great at it, and
2. Moms who aren't.

Don't feel guilty if you are the second type. I was too. Crafting does not come naturally to everyone. It can be overwhelming to think about the messes and expense. Sometimes it just seems easier to skip crafts. But your children will learn while they love you for letting them get messy, create, explore, and discover. These are the years to have fun with your child and experience the joy of being a parent.

After getting advice about what to buy and how to get organized from my friend, I plunged in head first. My kids responded in ways that I would never have imagined. My son, who was just 20 months when all this crafting began, amazed me with what he could do. He was able to glue on googly eyes all by himself. And he loved every second of it.

Now when it rains, I don't have to hold back my tears. I'm even a little excited to see what we will create and learn that day.

Teacher's Advice

Although it can seem overwhelming for moms, don't deprive your child, or yourself, from making crafts—which can become a creative process called art. In fact, offer your child numerous opportunities to express themselves through the process of art. It isn't the product that is important, according to many child development specialists and art therapists. It is the child's self-expression, which gives you a view of what is inside. Lucy isn't unique: All children love to make things showing their individuality and just for the pure enjoyment of creating. It gives them a sense of worth and confidence to spend time with family members while talking, expressing, and receiving praise. They feel connected, loved, and happy—which results in fewer behavior problems.

Many art teachers and therapists now consider the *process* much more important than the product. Art can be an outlet to express emotional trauma such as parents separating, a death, or bullying. Through art, a child can relax and communicate. How can your child not feel rushed when our world is on the fast-track for everything? Take a deep breath and let the creative therapy begin.

When children make a craft, they are developing:

- Creativity: Assembling something unique.
- Planning: Thinking, following through, finishing a project.
- Following Directions: Thinking in a sequence, reaching a desired result.
- Knowledge: Investigating their world by exploring textures and materials.
- Fine Motor Skills: Feeling, manipulating, sorting, arranging, pushing and placing objects.
- Exploration and Discovery: How things work and change like pouring glue, playdough formations, paint mixing.
- Language: Expression of how something feels, looks and smells; describing what was created and its purpose (if it has one, other than just

being fun and making one happy which is perfectly wonderful in itself).

- Sorting: Ordering, categorizing and cleaning up.
- Self-Esteem: Pride in finished project, sense of accomplishment.
- Family Play or Traditions: A sense of belonging, family connectivity, being valued and wanted.

A self-esteem booster is to proudly display your child's art or give it as a gift to grandparents who appreciate the thought, perhaps more than the product. But they will never tell your child that. They know it is precious in some fashion. Be careful not to stress over your child's product being perfect or looking exactly as you had envisioned. They are unique individuals who see things differently than you due to a lack of experience. Allowing children to be creative contributes to novel thoughts, problem-solving skills and entrepreneurs. The highest achievers in societies were encouraged, or at least allowed, to think outside the box. If they weren't, they stole the time to do it anyway, becoming great artists, writers and scientists. The next time you have the impulse to correct their art, think of Mark Zackerberg (Facebook), Bill Gates (Microsoft), Steve Jobs (Apple Computers), and Jeff Bezos (Amazon.com) or Stephen Spielberg (movie producer).

The Basics of Crafting

Don't forget, crafts do not have to be complicated. It is okay if you do not end up with something perfect that can be displayed at an art gallery for prodigy children. In fact, the best crafts are:

- Easy,
- Cheap, and
- FUN!

Where to Begin

First, you need to get organized. A good place to start is to go to your local hobby or department store and purchase some basics.

The **most** important point to remember is that you control everything. Keep all your supplies in a bag or tub in the closet and get them out one at a time. Put away a project completely before you allow a new one to be used. Do not dump everything and let your child choose what to do. They need guidance, modeling and boundaries. This educational play should be separated from their normal toys.

What to Purchase

- Colored construction paper
- Googly eyes
- Popsicle sticks
- Stickers of any kind
- Washable paint (buy big bottles in the primary colors of red, yellow and blue as a start)
- Small paintbrushes
- Playdough in several different colors (or make your own; see recipes below)
- Pipe cleaners
- Glue sticks
- White school glue
- Kid safety scissors
- Sand (the finer, the better)
- Buttons of various sizes, colors, shapes and textures
- Beads of varieties, sizes and shapes
- Colored rocks
- River-style rocks
- Colored Rice (see Chapter Two for recipe)
- Various pastas

- Large push-pins
- Ice cube trays
- Paper cups
- Long, sturdy shoe strings
- Funnels
- Muffin tins

Art supplies can be inexpensive, especially in the summer before school starts. It is a good idea to buy in bulk the items marked down and save them for that rainy day. Before tossing away anything, think: *What else can this be used for?* You will be amazed how many projects you can do with just construction paper, a toilet paper roll, and some googly eyes! Upcycle, Recycle, Reuse, Remake with:

- Rolls: Toilet paper, paper towel, gift paper, mailing tubes
- Plastic containers: Whipped topping, icing and yogurt containers (perfect for playdough)
- Boxes of various sizes: pizza, shoe, appliances
- Plastic drink bottles
- Eye droppers from medicine or vitamins
- Oatmeal and nut cardboard containers
- Milk jugs and containers
- Newspapers, magazines, comics, cards
- Craft scraps
- Veggie, cookie and meat trays

While you are shopping, purchase some bins and tubs. Keep everything in the tubs or in plastic bags. Some things, such as ice cube trays and paper towel rolls, may be too big for tubs. For these items, try using a soft recyclable bag because it will not tear.

Organizing is very important.

Here is an example tub for paint supplies. Keep your brushes in here so you don't lose them. When you offer paint, keep it very simple. Squeeze paint onto plastic or paper plates or even old egg cartons. Just put a dab of paint into each of the slots. Water soluble paint can be diluted with water to stretch it.

Here is one way to store playdough. Of course, you can also make homemade playdough (see Chapter Two).

Even if you choose to make your own playdough, you might want to invest in some store-bought playdough so you can re-use the containers for your own home-made playdough after the store version dries up. These small containers are a great way to keep playdough air-tight and to separate by color or for storing small craft objects in like googly eyes.

Now that you are organized, you are ready to start creative fun times with your child.

Be Prepared for Messes

Making reasonable messes is healthy. Some children like to do craft and art projects simply because they want to get messy. It's therapeutic. Depending on your tolerance to messes, the following will help:

- Never leave children unsupervised.
- Lay down newspapers, a plastic tablecloth or old shower curtain over craft surface.
- Have children wear an old t-shirt.

- Use washable paint, markers and glue.
- Water down glue and paint if you want to stretch out supplies.
- Add a drop or two of dish soap to paint before finger painting. It makes it easier to wash off.
- Keep wipes handy for fast cleaning of surfaces and children's hands so they don't put substances in their eyes.
- Remember, children like to help clean up messes—especially with praise. This teaches them responsibility.
- Leave time for cleaning up and bathing so you won't feel stressed over messes.

Accidents Will Happen

It would be interesting to see how many Google searches are made every day for: "How do I get playdough out of my carpet?" If you're careful, hopefully messes will be minimal, but it is inevitable that accidents will happen at some point.

Clean-up Tips:

- Remain calm and your children will too.
- The sooner the clean-up process begins—the easier to clean.
- Nail polish remover will remove non-washable craft paint on skin, as will long baths. Children love to soak in bubble baths with interesting floating objects, releasing tension and gradually the paint, especially with a sponge for scrubbing and added interest. *Always* supervise children around water.
- Acrylic craft paints are not easily removed from carpet. Immediately soak with hot water and scrub with a stiff brush, repeating process. Water soluble paints are easier to remove.

- Playdough is not easily removed from carpet. Do not use hot water or cleaning solutions, but allow it to dry completely and then loosen with a stiff brush. It may be necessary to vacuum clean or wash with gentle soap and then cold water. You may need to repeat the process. A stain remover may be applied if a color stain is left in the carpet. It takes time, but you can often pull the playdough from the carpet after it dries. If the carpet strands are long, you may be able to cut it out without leaving evidence.
- Toothpaste will remove permanent marker. Leave on five minutes before scrubbing.
- Shaving cream removes crayon marks and kills germs. Children enjoy scrubbing crayon marks off with shaving cream. Add a scent or a few drops of food coloring for more interest. Give them a sponge or wipe and let them work their muscles. Compliment them for their help.
- Water diluted with vinegar removes odors and some stains and works wonders for those wet towels and washcloths that have sat too long in the washer.
- For Little Diva's: Nail polish remover will not remove nail polish from carpet. Paint nails over a towel or on easy-to-clean surface. Keep nail polish out of the reach of children. They want to model you, after all.

Craft Ideas for Home

Children get so much more out of crafts if you can base them around a theme, such as Christmas or Valentine's Day, or even better, around a favorite book. You will see your child develop a stronger interest in books when you create something special with them that has relevance. Let them paint the story on paper or even rocks. This is an inexpensive and interesting way for them to retell the story in their own words or form of expression. Then you will be able to know how much they understood about the book.

The Very Hungry Caterpillar

Cut an egg carton in half and let your child glue on googly eyes. They will need to hold the eyes on while they dry which promotes patience. Next cut a pipe cleaner in half, fold together and push into the egg carton. Bend the ends to make an antennae. Now, let your child paint the caterpillar. Before you know it, voila! You have some very hungry caterpillars (from the book *The Very Hungry Caterpillar* by Eric Carle)

Five Silly Turkeys by Salina Yoon

This is a fun rhyming book especially good to read during the Fall. Help your child make a Thankful Turkey. Use an old coffee can or any container with a lid. Glue brown construction paper around it and they can glue feathers and googly eyes on the turkey. You could even cut a slit in the top, write thankful notes every day, and drop them in the container. Or encourage your children to draw pictures on small pieces of paper expressing what they are thankful for, printing their words on the back. They can fold the paper and push it into the can for fine motor development. Read the notes on Thanksgiving Day encouraging gratitude in your children and showing appreciation for their acts of kindness.

Crafts as Gifts

Painting

Buy a wooden figurine, bird house, or something of significance and let the kids paint it for a personalized gift. They will enjoy painting and decorating the object perhaps by adding some glue to the paint and then shaking baking sprinkles on top. Make sure they know who they are painting it for. You might even consider taking a photo of them painting it and include the photo in the gift so that Grandma knows how hard they worked. Children also love painting ceramic Christmas ornaments. Acrylic paints last longer than water-based paints, but close supervision is necessary when using non-washable substances. Help your child write their name on the back with the date or do it for them, bragging about their artistry.

Fossil Dough

Mix 4 cups flour, 1 cup salt, and 1 and ½ cups water. Your child will enjoy pouring the ingredients into a bowl, kneading and adding a few drops of food coloring and even scent. You will likely need to add more water, but mix it together and see what happens. It should stick together, but not be too runny. Now you can do all kinds of things with this. You can roll it flat and make handprints or footprints. You can roll balls and make a snowman. Let children use cookie cutters or objects to make different shapes and then decorate them with beads, raisins, pipe cleaners, or anything you have handy at home. After you are finished creating, the dough will harden into something you can keep around the house on display, or give as a gift.

Toilet paper holder crafts

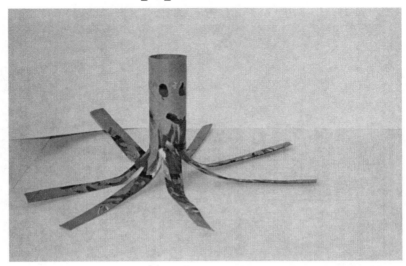

Never throw away toilet paper rolls! Your children can make monsters by gluing construction paper around it, then gluing on googly eyes, pipe cleaners, noses, or whatever they find workable, even pieces of tissue or construction paper they have cut into small pieces. They can make creatures like an octopus, bird or kitty cat—whatever their imagination and hands desire to create.

Painting with Straws

Mix a little water and water-soluble paint into several different squeeze bottles. Offer a large white sheet of paper and let your child squeeze small amounts of paint onto the paper. You may want to have children practice *blowing* into a bowl of water first, making bubbles, before blowing through the straws to paint, so that they understand "blow" not "suck." Demonstrate how to blow out air to make the paint fly across the page. The paper will end up with all the different splashes of color if you use the primary colors of red, yellow and blue. Once your child gets the hang of it, they might even be able to blow bubbles!

It is better to create than to learn! Creating is the essence of life. ~ Julius Caesar

Chapter Four
Playing Inside

Mommy's Dilemma

Surgeons are typically very good under pressure and although my husband is still in training, he is no different. He was perfect when my daughter was a colicky baby. Her frantic screams didn't faze him one bit. He patiently worked and worked until he figured out how to rock her, soothe her, and get her to stop crying. However, as my daughter got older it became apparent that he was having difficulty transitioning from a world of scalpels to a world of dolls and teddy bears.

When my daughter was about two, he tried to ask our daughter about her day and have real adult conversations with her, It never worked. I could tell they wanted to bond, but they were both confused about what to do. On top of this, my daughter was starting to get wild. It was cold and wet outside so playing outdoors wasn't fun for anyone. She clearly wasn't getting enough exercise so she was starting to act out and be naughty.

One day I suggested he chase her around and play tag with her. He truly looked shocked. He had never spent any time with toddlers and it literally never entered his mind that a two-year-old could play tag. He started chasing her around the room and she shrieked with excitement.

That night, she asked Daddy to put her to bed, which made him beam with pride. From that point forward, they started playing together and their world completely changed.

Teacher's Advice

Children are born to play. As we saw with Lucy, knowing how to play is intuitive for children and it is their form of exercise and learning. When your child is moving, exploring, using several senses, or trying things out in various ways, brain connections are developing and learning is taking place. Your preschooler needs to *participate* in activities; simply watching others do things, or viewing screens, isn't enough. Ample research documents that there is more brain activity taking place during active play than compared to passive observation. The brain also needs trial and error experiences as well as much repetition in fun and interesting ways for learning to be retained. All of this is provided through playful games and activities. Play also offers opportunities to learn social skills and build vocabulary as well as motor skills. When children play with parents or other children, they learn about relationships, how to work together, and how to become a productive, happy person.

Studies show that children who don't get enough physical activity will begin to show a lack in optimal gross and fine motor skill development.

On top of the skills and health benefits from playing and exercising, there is the behavioral component to be considered. Exercise and unstructured outdoor playtime can help alleviate mood disorders in children. Hard physical exercise leads children to be more focused and be in a more relaxed mental state. Children need for their bodies to gain a sense of balance, coordination, and motor abilities. These skills are learned by getting off the couch, chasing other kids around, exploring their fascinating world, and using their little bodies to try to accomplish a goal. This chapter is designed to offer ideas for developing muscles and brain power regardless of the weather.

Indoor Activities

Fetch
Kids can be just like dogs. They love to run after things. As soon as toddlers can walk, they enjoy going after a ball. This fun doesn't diminish much as they get older. Go into a carpeted room or at least one that is long and relatively obstacle-free. Throw the ball to the end and tell your children to run and get the ball for you and bring it back. Be really excited when they bring it to you. Young children also enjoy taking objects to other people, which develops following instructions and language skills.

Trampoline
Don't get scared, you don't have to buy a real trampoline. Learning to jump is a real challenge for young children and is a great way to work on gross motor skills. If you have an old mattress, place it next to a wall, ideally on carpet. If you are worried about the appearance of it, try putting it in a basement if you have one, or somewhere out of the way. Then let the kids go to town. Get on and jump with them. You may think you don't have the energy, but your adrenaline will increase if you'll try it and you'll release endorphins—the "feel good" hormones. Put on some music to inspire you. This is a great workout! Hold hands with them as they jump while yelling "Wheeeeeee!" Shouting "Wheeeeee!" is not mandatory but your children will love you for it. And you will be burning calories as your children admire your abilities and participation.

Hide and Seek
Kids aren't great at this game until they are around four, but they really love it even starting at a younger age. Don't be surprised if they yell, "Here I am,

Mommy! I'm under the table!" Even though they don't understand, it is great practice for them to take turns and also to learn patience while they wait for you to find them. When it's your turn to hide, don't make it too hard. They'll lose interest if they can't find you soon. You may have to make a little noise. Use animated facial expressions to show your surprise and delight at them finding you.

Find the "Blueberries"

This game works well once your child is about two and a half. It's like a Scavenger or Easter Egg Hunt. You'll need some Pom-poms from your local craft store. Children like the bright colored ones best. You'll also need a few buckets or baskets. Explain that they will wait in one room while you hide the "blueberries." While they are waiting, throw the Pom-poms everywhere. Again, don't make it too hard or they will lose interest. Just put them on the top of chairs, tables, or under tables with part sticking out. Then tell them to come find everything. They will scurry around the room looking for all the blueberries. This game teaches patience and also helps children learn to take turns. It burns up energy and can be played with multiple children. Vary the game using different objects. You could also add difficulty by having them count the number of blueberries they found at the end or sort the pompoms by color. *Note* Keep an eye on younger children for choking hazard.

Jump on Couch Pillows

If you really care about your furniture, this game probably isn't for you. However, if you're looking for something to do inside to burn energy, this is a great one. Take all the pillows off the couch and place them a few inches apart. Show the kids how to jump from pillow to pillow. You could also take both hands and swing your child so that they land on the pillows. They might even like to run across the pillows. Be careful that the pillows aren't close to any tables or sharp objects, as children often lose their balance while playing this game.

Build a Fort

Drape blankets over chairs, ottomans or couches. Make a fort or tent. Give your kids things to take into the fort and maybe even go with them. Ask them to bring books to read inside the fort. Girls will often want to put their babies "to sleep" inside the fort. Looking at books with a flashlight adds interest.

Simon Says

This is a great game if you've had a long day and want the kids to burn energy but are too tired for tag. Simon says, "Touch your toes!" Simon says, "Say Yipeee!" Simon says, "Do a Dance!" Maybe they have some suggestions they can say to each other, giving you a break to just watch and supervise when needed.

Pretend to be Animals

Show your little one how to jump like a frog, walk like an elephant, or slither like a snake. Then ask them to do each one. Be creative. For animals that don't do anything exciting, like a cow, imitate the sounds that they make. Sing "Old McDonald Had a Farm."

Wrestle

There is nothing better for burning energy than good old-fashioned wrestling. Let your children tackle you and act surprised. Or get on the floor on your hands and knees and tell them to get on your back—like they're riding a horse. Give piggy-back rides that end with them being thrown (gently) onto the couch and tickled. The book *Parenting with Love and Logic* by Fay and Cline explains how there is no better way to bond with your children than by getting on the floor with them. Moms can wrestle too! Kids need to touch parents and be touched and tickled by their parents. Laughing is contagious and remembered.

Tag

Kids really love to be chased. Sometimes you can just run slowly after them and run in circles 20 times. They won't care that they haven't actually been tagged. Just the thrill of being chased is enough for them. This is a wonderful way to burn some energy out of them while you are burning calories too.

Music

Play music and dance with your child or march together. Play "follow the leader." Have your child copy everything you do when you jump, slide, and clap. Let your child lead you with their ideas or patterns while listening to music. Performing simple patterns enhances reading and math skills as does singing chants that rhyme while jumping rope.

Children enjoy playing with bells which can be bought at craft stores and strung for a necklace or bracelet. They like to bang on pots and pans, tap sticks to the musical beat, and sing rhyming chants loudly *and* softly. There are many benefits to music including:

- Songs can teach numbers, letters, or build memory and vocabulary;
- Learning music enhances creativity, resourcefulness, and playing with a language;
- Music develops listening skills;
- Children learn to cooperate while bonding with a larger group; and
- Music fosters math and reading skills through repetitive patterns in songs or dance.

Children love to make and decorate a shaker. They could paint a tube or plastic bottle or decorate it using stickers. Or they could wrap it with pipe cleaners or yarn before filling it. Encourage your child to find different things to put in the shaker to produce soft or louder sounds such as:

- Quiet Rattles: Sand, salt, sugar, confetti, cotton balls, Pom-poms, paper pieces, cotton swabs and pasta
- Louder Rattles: Paper clips, small pebbles, birdseed, beads, beans, rice, buttons, coins, dried beans, buttons

The Freeze Game

Put on some music and start dancing! Then, stop the music and yell "Freeze!" The kids will enjoy being frozen in all kinds of interesting poses. Start the music again and repeat. It's helpful to explain the rules before you start this game, since it's probably something they've never done before.

The Silent Game

Most people probably remember doing this game as a child. See who can stay silent the longest. Preschoolers don't last long, but love to try. And what parent doesn't love some quiet time?

Rope or String Play

Tie a rope across two chairs and tie things onto the rope. You could cut foam into shapes, then cut the edge to the middle, cutting out a circle. Your child will enjoy putting the shapes onto the rope and sliding them across the room on the rope. Or string beads or pinwheel macaroni on a long string and tie it across the room. You child will benefit from moving objects on the string which helps develop both fine and large muscles.

Imaginary/Fantasy Play

Blocks, action figures, dolls, forts or dollhouses made out of large cardboard boxes give children opportunities to use their imagination, fantasize, imitate, model, and develop their unique personality. Assemble "Make-Believe" collections into boxes with old clothes—dresses, shirts. Add purses, shoes, hats and boas to the mix. Put together a collection of oven mitts, balls, caps, and baseball cards. Another good collection would include old kitchen pots, pans and utensils, along with play food for hours of enjoyment. Wash cans and use empty food containers so they can play "kitchen" or "grocery store" by adding play money. Put out paper, crayons, old phones and broken computers to play office. You may hear them repeat your words as they are on the phone, or talk to imaginary friends, giving you an insight as to what they are thinking. Uninterrupted imaginative time is important for their development. Organize items into theme boxes and rotate them so that they stay out of sight for a couple of months. They will seem like new when you get them down on a rainy day.

Parents are not interested in justice, they're interested in peace and quiet ~ Bill Cosby

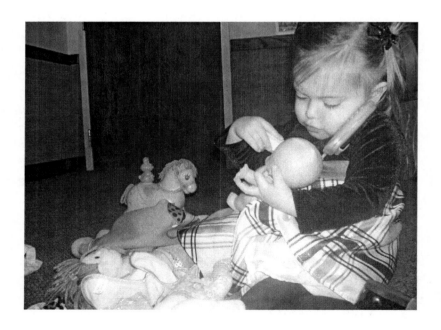

Chapter Five
Playing Outside

Mommy's Dilemma

A few days after we moved into our new house, our doorbell rang. Obviously, I was expecting a new neighbor. What I wasn't expecting was a five-year-old, all alone, asking if our daughter could come out to play. I was very shocked that a parent would allow their child to run around the neighborhood alone at 7:00 p.m. What kind of parent does that? Don't they know the rate of kidnappings in this country? Not to mention the risk of getting hit by a car. That day I made the decision that I would be very vigilant about always being outside with my children and never leaving them alone for even a second.

Shortly after this, when my daughter was about three, something happened that made me question my decision. One day a few older girls knocked on the front door and asked her to play. Lucy, my daughter, hurried outside and everything was fun for about 15 minutes until suddenly the two older girls started whispering and ran away together, leaving Lucy behind. My daughter looked confused then took off after them. They kept ignoring her and she didn't understand why. In order to get their attention, she started hitting them and running away, like she was trying to play tag. Unfortunately, this really irritated them. She walked up to one of the girls and hit her playfully and the girl threw her to the ground. The neighbor girl put both legs and arms and all her strength into it. It literally looked like a football tackle.

I ran to the girls and was mad as a hornet. I demanded that the girl tell me why she had thrown Lucy to the ground. "She deserved it," the girl told me. "She was hitting me."

I was the only parent outside at the time and I lectured all the girls on playing nicely together, but I could tell the older girl was making fun of me. Suddenly, I became panicked that Lucy would be even more ostracized. I could imagine the girl taunting Lucy and saying, "Lucy, your mom is mean."

Later when we were inside, I asked my daughter why she was hitting the girls. She answered, "I was trying to be funny, Mom." At that point I was forced to admit that maybe my daughter did need to be taught a lesson, by someone other than her mom. She needed to learn that if she hits people, she may get thrown to the ground, Karate Kid style.

A few days after the throw-down, those same girls asked my daughter to play with them. I observed from a distance and was so excited to see that Lucy didn't hit anyone. Instead, they invented their own imaginative game where my daughter was the "baby" and she was supposed to run around and say "goo goo gaga." One of the older girls was the mommy and the other was the daddy. The big girls read stories to my daughter and Lucy was so thrilled to run around after them and be part of the group. In turn, I was thrilled to see that Lucy really did learn a lesson from her friends and wasn't any worse for the wear.

Teacher's Advice

The lesson Lucy learned that day from her friend will be remembered far longer than the lecture she would have gotten from her mom. She learned that her friends don't think it's funny when she hits them. She learned a lesson in democracy and was rewarded. Now when she becomes a Kindergartener, she will know that it is not okay to hit other kids while trying to be funny. This is one lesson every child should know *before* they enter school, for everyone's benefit.

Hara Marano wrote the book *A Nation of Wimps*. Lenore Skenazy wrote *Free-Range Kids*. Marano and Skenazy have long observed and chronicled the decline of free play in the United States, meaning unsupervised outdoor play, and have compiled years of research. This quote is taken from *The American Journal of Play* when they were interviewed:

"By playing regularly with other kids—playing freely—kids gain social skills that become a natural deterrent to bullying. They learn how to handle disruptions. They learn how to negotiate disputes... and how to be assertive.... Kids need to play outdoors where they have space to explore and run around. Also, playing in the dirt seems to strengthen the immune system. Without free outdoor play, kids lack the ability to gather and play spontaneously, and that in turn causes a serious lack of social skills. Gathering and playing freely with others lets kids practice many aspects of democracy and when free play is denied, so are these opportunities."

Indeed, according to ample research, children today who don't have the chance to play outside have a tendency to be more depressed and ridden with anxiety. As a parent, it is so important to make the effort to take your children outside and actually engage them once you get there. You'll be able to exercise with them and they will think you are a really cool mom playing outdoor games with them, swinging at the park, even sliding down a slide. Of course, you don't want to leave babies unattended, but long stroller walks are also an enjoyable way of connecting with nature and your children. Talk, listen, and answer their numerous questions about a world they are newly discovering.

How Children Benefit From Playing Outside

- People are social. We crave friendships for support, learning, and experiencing closeness to others. Electronic gadgets do not communicate back to a child, nor do they listen and answer their many questions.
- Learning to play outdoor games uses creativity, imagination and brain power by making up new games and participating in sports and games that have been around for decades.
- Children are curious about everything. They learn by exploring and discovering using their five senses. They need opportunities to smell, touch, taste, see and hear different things in our environment including the dirty/messy stuff such as water puddles, rain, snow, and mud. Look for cold or rainy weather apparel at garage sales, community thrift stores or when on sale so you will be prepared and can have fun in most weather conditions.
- Playing outside develops strong bones, helps prevent obesity, works muscles, and improves mood by producing endorphins (the feel good hormone) with prolonged physical activity.
- Humans need sunlight. Many people are vitamin D deficient and don't even know it. If you are worried about skin cancer then use sunscreen and wear a hat, long sleeves and pants.
- Playing outside strengthens the immune system. When children play in dirt or touch bugs, they are building up their immune system naturally to things in our environment.
- Peace and quiet will be appreciated. Have children listen for sounds in the stillness: Birds, crickets, wind, rustling leaves, feet splashing in

water, or just enjoy the quietness of nature with no commercials bombarding your mind.

- We are part of nature and playing outside develops an appreciation of our earth and the creatures inhabiting it.
- Childhood memories will be built from making neighborhood friends, which creates a sense of community and belonging.

As we saw in Lucy's case, the less that her mom interfered with childish squabbles, the better, especially with the older kids. However, we can't abandon common sense. An adult should ALWAYS be present outdoors with young children. There is no excuse for letting your five-year-old go outside alone to "find something to do." Times have changed and we can't ignore the fact that there are bad people out there. However, find a way to make sure the kids are safe without interfering. Read a book from the porch or someplace where you can see them and make sure strangers aren't lurking. When you hear a car, look up and make sure all the kids are safely out of the way. If other moms are outside, chat with them, but from a distance to give your child opportunities to socialize and build relationships with other children.

Of course, sometimes the neighbors are busy. Or maybe you live on a street without any young children. Now what? Use this time to bond with your children. Put down your book or techno gadgets and enjoy the outdoors while you create lasting memories. They will love you for it and everyone will be healthier and happier. Even if friends are available, sometimes children need encouragement and ideas on what to do. Make an effort to try a new idea each week or even every day! Listen to your child's ideas and join in their joy of discovery and play.

Outside Play

Sidewalk Chalk

Almost all children enjoy sidewalk chalk. This is a perfect opportunity to foster creativity. Let children draw whatever they want and ask them questions about what they have drawn. Have your child lie down and trace around their body. Then they can fill in the rest. If they are interested, print their name and have them trace the letters in different colors. Remember to capitalize only the first letter in their name to help their future teachers.

Hopscotch

Draw a simple hopscotch pattern which is one square, then two squares on top of that, then one square and continue the pattern. Draw numbers 1 through 10 using sidewalk chalk. Have your child toss a small rock on one of the squares. Can they hop to it (one foot, then two feet, then one foot) while bending over to pick up the rock while balancing on one foot?

There are other ways to play hopscotch so that various ages of children can make use of the game and be challenged. Make a game of finding rocks and ask your child to put one rock on the number one. Then put two rocks on the number two and so on. Try this with leaves, acorns, seeds or other interesting outdoor objects. They could trace over the numbers connecting the number/object concept. If your children become frustrated or bored with specific rules, just hop around and sing and be grateful for the laughter, fun and closeness you will experience.

Hopscotch promotes:
- Sharing and taking turns
- Following directions and learning rules to a game
- Number recognition
- Counting and sequencing
- Concept of the meaning of numbers

- Physical exercise of hopping, balancing and jumping
- Cognitive development: Expression of language and linear thinking to reach a desired outcome
- Cooperation and good sportsmanship: Playing a gentle but competitive game
- Confidence: Praise of accomplishments encourages an "I Can Do It" attitude.

Tag and Hide-and-Seek

Older kids love to initiate these games, which are great for burning energy. Sometimes it is necessary to remind children not to be too rough, to be considerate of others and to include everyone in the game.

Scavenger Hunt

If you plan ahead, this can be a really fun way to spend an afternoon. You could use a Word document or draw pictures for clues for non-readers. It is best to print the word beside the picture to foster letter connections. Basic things you might find are leaves, rocks, pinecones, twigs, bugs, shadows. Then go on a scavenger hunt to find all the pieces. Children love to mark off lists, modeling their parents. They would enjoy carrying a basket for their treasures, their list and a marker or pencil.

Feeding the Birds, Visiting Ponds

Let the children throw out bread crumbs and watch the birds flock around. If you live near a pond, take some bread down by the water. It won't take much encouragement for the kids to throw bread to ducks, frogs or turtles. Children also love to throw rocks into water. They are using large muscles and their senses to see and hear what happens as well as experiencing gravity and velocity. Does the rock make ripples when thrown into the water? Perhaps some children can make rocks skip on the water when thrown sideways like a Frisbee.

Read Coinciding Books before or after a Walk

Read books to coincide with activities so children can make the reading/environment connection. Children love books about animals and science (our world). They could collect rocks and later paint "stories" on the rocks even re-telling about their adventurous day. Sequencing would be learned if the story rocks were placed in order of events. Listening to your child's story will give you a glimpse into their reality or imagination. Helping them express themselves or know the names of things you saw builds their vocabulary. Memories of outdoor family or neighborhood play may be among the fondest remembered as your child matures.

Walks Can Be Fun and Meaningful

- Discover different types of plants, trees, flowers, and critters. You may want to collect things for sorting and patterning later. Visit the library and bring home books about nature and critters so your child can make the reading/learning-about-our-world connection.

- Race to the next street and STOP at the stop sign pointing out environmental print has meaning.
- Sing songs.
- Move in patterns.
- Be really quiet as you tip-toe and listen for sounds.
- Talk about how you are feeling that very minute and encourage your children to express their feelings. Children who learn that they can come to you with any problem will have fewer problems when they are older, or at least know that you welcome knowing about their problems and want to help.
- Teach children to respect our earth. With encouragement, young children can help pick up litter. Nature collages build memory and can be a fun sensory project.
- Collect seeds and plant them when the season is right.

Carriages, Wagons, Tricycles, Scooters, Bicycles

Children are often impressed when they see Mom and Dad riding bikes. It must be surprising for them to find out that mom and dad are coordinated enough! When young children observe their parents doing something that they are unable to do, it gives them the desire to learn because they love, admire and imitate their family members more than anybody else. A child carrier attached to your bike will allow your child to safely enjoy a bike ride while observing the great outdoors, feeling the wind, hearing new sounds, and relaxing with the people they love the most. Make sure their helmet fits correctly. A more expensive investment would be the covered "stage coach" that is pulled behind a bike. A Craigslist find might provide an affordable price. Of course, the child will not be benefiting from much movement or exercise but they will enjoy the ride and might take a nap, giving you some down time.

Simon Says

Kick back in a comfy chair and play Simon says, then watch the neighborhood kids join the fun. Get really silly with "Simon's" suggestions and enjoy the children's giggles.

Follow the Leader

Participate in the first round of follow-the-leader demonstrating how to jump like a frog, hop like a bunny, run in a circle, swing arms like an elephant trunk, hop on one leg, or whatever they will enjoy and are capable of doing or learning. Then encourage them to take turns and think of their own movement that they'd like the others to imitate.

An adult can also initiate movement with repeated patterns such as: Jump/jump/touch head or slide/slide/hop. Children love the "bunny hop" especially around Easter. Form a line and tell them to hold onto the person's waist who is in front of them. Then everyone hops to the front, hops to the back, then hops, hops, hops forward and repeats. Or play "hokey pokey" teaching body parts.

For some reason, holding hands, going in a circle and chanting "Ring around the Rosey" is hysterical to children. It must be because it is just plain fun to be silly, feel included, and to fall down and roll around or kick legs up in the air.

Ring around the Rosey
Pocket full of Posey
Ashes, Ashes
We all fall down.

Jump Rope

It takes time and practice for most children to learn how to jump rope. Begin with a long rope and gently swing the rope to the sides for a child to jump over before going in large circles. It is fun for the children to learn chants while jumping rope. Substantial research documents that rhyming, rhythm, and repetition help children learn reading and math skills. Here is a favorite from the book *Miss Mary Mack*.

Miss Mary Mack, Mack, Mack
All dressed in black, black, black
With silver buttons, buttons, buttons
All down her back, back, back
She asked her mother, mother, mother
For fifty cents, cents, cents
To see the elephant, elephant, elephant
Jump the fence, fence, fence
She jumped so high, high, high
She touched the sky, sky, sky
And didn't come back, back, back
Till the fourth of July, July, July

Water Activities

Children love being in wading pools pouring water from cups and buckets. Gravity is fascinating for young children. Sprinklers and slippery slides can provide hours of entertainment and exercise. Give an 18-month-old boy a sprinkler on a low setting and he'll be busy for hours and end up either clean or muddy, but happy and ready for a good night's sleep.

Balls

Ever wonder how many balls have been played with on this earth and with how many different games? Cavemen were probably tossing round rocks or apples playing games with clubs. Children love balls from a very early age and the fascination seems to continue throughout adulthood. We've all heard, "It's as American as baseball and apple pie." Children will spend hours tossing balls into a bucket or box, or rolling and kicking them.

Buy a used croquet set. You don't need to follow the rules. Just try to keep it fun. Put the metal loops wherever you think the kids can manage to hit the balls through and point them toward the goal.

Balloons

For some reason, balloons seem to signify fun and importance. Children love balloons for tossing and smacking. Water balloons are always a favorite at parties. Older children enjoy holding onto the ends of a beach towel and tossing water balloons into the air trying to catch them on the way down without them rolling off the towel.

Imagination/Fantasy/Pretend Play

Children learn to be creative, think, imitate, model, and explore all kinds of possibilities with imagination or free play (open-ended). Little boys love to be cowboys, warriors, heroes and daddies. Little girls love to be fairies, princesses or mommies.

Build a fort, dollhouse or tree house, if possible. If not, then ask your local home center or other store that sells appliances if you may have a large box. They will be thrilled to give it to you or call you when one becomes available. Let children decorate the box making it into anything they desire. You'll be impressed at how happy it makes a child to take ownership of their new play area, designing it with their unique creativity. Perhaps it could also be used as a special reading area with a little encouragement and a flashlight.

Hula Hoops

There are so many activities that can be done with Hula Hoops besides spinning them around your waist. Spin hoops around arms or roll a hoop on the ground and run after it having races. For a quieter activity, place a hoop flat on the ground and play marbles. Or put several hoops on the ground for sorting objects like rocks, leaves, sticks or whatever interests the child. Talk about same and different concepts.

Gardening

Gardening, whether flowers or vegetables, gives a child a sense of accomplishment and scientific discovery. You could start sprouts from seeds inside the house then plant them when the time is right. Children love watching bean seeds sprout in a plastic bag. Just spray the seeds every day with water and tape the bag on the window for sunlight. Or put seeds in cups filled with dirt and remind the children to water them daily. It is still a marvelous wonder how a tiny seed can grow into something you can eat, or into a large tree.

Finding worms and bugs in the earth can be delightful for young children, although perhaps not as welcomed by adults. The worms could be used for fishing with dad, giving moms a much needed break. You may find your child more fascinated by a simple wiggly worm than an expensive swing set.

We don't stop playing because we grow old; we grow old because we stop playing. ~ George Bernard Shaw

Chapter Six
Nurturing Yourself so You Can Nurture Your Children

Mommy's Dilemma

My second child, Jacob, had problems nursing. I finally had to pump the milk first, *then* feed him a bottle, which took over an hour for the whole process.

Lucy was only 20 months at the time. She began to feel neglected since Jacob had to be fed eight times per day and it took an hour each feeding. Things gradually got worse and worse until one day she learned how to unplug the breast pump. Jacob was screaming because he was hungry, but the pump could only work so fast.

Lucy got a devilish grin on her face and was delighted when she realized that she could control the breast pump from the wall.

I tried to reason with her, "Honey, please stop doing that. It's very dangerous and I need to get the milk out so I can feed the baby. Then he'll stop crying."

She stopped for a minute, but then couldn't help herself. She did it over and over again. I could feel my blood beginning to boil and suddenly I'd never been so angry in my life. I threw down the bottles and ran after her. I grabbed her by the arm and dragged her into timeout, screaming at her the whole time.

My anger dissolved as quickly as it came and I was ashamed and guilty for becoming so angry with my daughter. She suddenly seemed so little and helpless. I wanted to hug her, apologize and explain everything to her, but I knew a two-year-old would not understand. It was up to me to control my temper. But how?

Teacher's Advice

Sometimes nothing seems to work. Children get that evil grin on their face and you know they are going to do everything they can think of to be naughty and irritate you and their siblings. However, losing your temper only makes things worse.

There is now scientific evidence that backs this up. A study was recently released in *Proceedings of the National Academy of Sciences* which studied two groups of children and their mothers. They were put in a frustrating situation. The mothers and children were left in a small room that had a shiny package on the table. They were told that they could open the package, but only after the mother filled out all the forms. The mothers had no idea they were being watched. Based on the behavior of the mothers, everyone was categorized into two groups. The following was observed: Half of the mothers either ignored their child or harshly scolded them. The other half were more nurturing and explained patiently to the children why they couldn't open the package yet.

They waited several years and brought everyone back for MRI scans. The study showed that children with nurturing mothers had a larger hippocampus (area of the brain that controls short-term and long-term memory) by almost 10 percent than the children whose mothers tended to scold in a harsh manner.

This means that we, as parents, really do have an influence on the development of children. There is real responsibility in that knowledge. Researchers of this study do stress that occasionally losing your temper won't cause the hippocampus to suddenly shrink, but the study clearly shows how important it is to be nurturing. Do your best not to yell and scream at your child. Verbal abuse can be as harmful as physical abuse and can have long-lasting results as well. It affects your child's self-esteem. Never hit a child. You are bigger than they are. It doesn't work. It only teaches them to hit others and you may be creating a rebellious child.

Instead, if you find yourself at your wit's end, try closing your eyes and breathing deeply. Then try a little self-talk: "I am the adult. I am a role model. I teach respect. I love my kids and they love me."

Try a little whistling or sing your favorite tune—really loud. Or start smiling (even if it is fake). Smiling and laughing are contagious and makes it hard to stay mad. Sometimes children act naughty just to grab your attention or to get a rise out of you. If you act unbothered, they may lose interest.

Put the incident into perspective. Take a few deep breaths and ask yourself these questions:

- What difference will this make a year from now?
- Can I let it go or let my child have his way?
- How is this making my child feel?
- How will I feel about this tomorrow?

The Importance of Mommy Pampering

Another way to be a more nurturing mother is to nurture yourself. You've been busy all day being a teacher, mother, wife, sister, daughter, and role model. You've changed diapers, cooked, cleaned, and been expected to be a walking encyclopedia on every subject. Maybe you even went to work all day. Now self-pampering is required to prepare you for the next day of monumental and heroic tasks.

It is okay to put the kids to bed early. In fact, research shows that kids under six years old need to be asleep no later than eight o'clock and probably even earlier. After the kids go to sleep, take at least 15 minutes of uninterrupted alone time if this is at all possible. If this is not possible, then take at least 30 minutes of "No Questions Now" time. You've answered questions all day concerning why that toy isn't working to why having cookies for breakfast is not okay. You deserve to free your mind and body of demands. Light a scented candle and take deep breaths smelling the fragrance repeating, "I am special, too. I work hard. I deserve some quiet time. I need to focus on what is important in life." What really matters the most in your life? Who really cares the most about you? What makes you happy?

Splurge and buy yourself a foot whirlpool from a beauty supply business. Put some Epson salts in warm water with a little perfume or smelling salts. Or buy detoxifying salts from a health food store.

If you have a secret guilty pleasure, do it! It might be watching *The Bachelor* while you scroll through Pinterest. It might be reading *US Weekly* while you have a cup of tea in the morning. It might be walking around alone at the mall for an hour. Whatever it is, **don't feel guilty**. We are still people and we still need time for ourselves. Find a way to make it happen.

Exercise

Take a walk, ride a bike, do Pilates or Yoga. Exercising is doing something solely to benefit you. It is alright to take this time for yourself and necessary for your mental and physical health. Taking a walk in nature will bring you spiritual strength. Put your life into perspective. Think of eternity. Our time on earth is short. *Every day is a gift.*

Focus on the Positive

Think of all the many ways you are blessed to live in this country. We have running water, freedom, ample food and shelter. You may want to take Oprah's recommendation to keep a "Blessings" journal. Or have a "Blessings" jar. Keep paper and pens nearby. When something wonderful happens, write it down. You can read the notes when you are feeling depressed or at wits-end. Encourage other family members to contribute writings to the jar. Your child could draw a picture of what made them happy and you could write a few words on the back. Probably something that made your child happy involved you; it will be uplifting to read it later.

Kitchen Cures

Remedies from the kitchen are cheap and easily available. Here are some ways to pamper yourself from inexpensive ingredients in your kitchen.

Egg yolk facial: Separate the yolk from the white and spread it on your face. This dries quickly, tightening the face and leaving it very clean. Or use the whites in the same way to see which you like better. Separate the egg and put it in small jars. You can store them in the refrigerator and it will stay fresh for several days. You have given yourself an organic facial for pennies.

Honey Do's. Do put honey on your face. It softens the skin. Of course, it is sticky and needs to be washed off eventually. But it feels tingly as honey works its miracles. Try sitting in the sun as the honey warms. You can put honey on your hands, elbows and feet to soften those dry areas. A dab of honey on a blemish heals the spot rapidly because honey kills bacteria.

Beanie Back Bag. Sew a long piece of material on three sides (5" x 12"). Fill it with hard beans and sew the last side (or buy one at a bath store). Heat it in the microwave for a warm back massager. This also feels good behind your neck to relax those tight muscles. These make wonderful gifts for your tired friends who have preschoolers or for your child's preschool teacher.

Drink "antioxidant" drinks instead of sodas. Grocery and health food stores carry an assortment of herbal and antioxidant beverages. Always have a healthy drink available, especially water. Water is your body's principal chemical component and makes up about 60 percent of your body weight. Every system in your body depends on water. Use the "8 x 8 rule" or drink eight 8-ounce glasses of fluids a day (about 1.9 liters). Offer your children more water instead of sugared juice. Put a little lemon in it for flavor, which also acts as a natural cleanser and has Vitamin C. Take a multivitamin at the very least. Many people in our society are deficient in Vitamin D which is a mood elevator. Vitamin C and E will help build up your immune system and can prevent viruses attacking your body.

Showers for Mom

Every mom deserves the luxury of a shower without someone whining outside the shower door. Try to find this time for yourself, whether it's while the kids are taking a nap or while you leave dad in charge for 30 minutes. If you cannot make it happen during the day, consider waking before the kids get out of bed. This might seem silly, especially for moms who stay at home, but try it. It will seem very luxurious to have the house all to yourself so that you can shower alone, have a cup of coffee, or maybe just relax for a few minutes before the crazy day begins. That way you won't start the day already feeling behind. Try and wake up at least 30 minutes before the kids usually awaken, so that you aren't rushing. That hurried feeling is contagious and not appreciated by little ones nor is it healthy.

Naps

Take a nap when your child is napping. Share a book to help your child fall asleep, then sleep some yourself. Even a 15-minute snooze can work wonders.

Time with Friends

Research shows there are numerous health benefits to having nurturing and meaningful relationships with other women. Take the time to call your friends. Schedule a lunch or dinner or even a Girls' Night Out. Consider joining or creating a book club. Don't feel guilty for needing some "adult time." This will only make you a better mom.

The beauty of a woman is not in a facial mole but is reflected in her soul. It is the caring that she lovingly gives, the passion that she shows. True beauty grows with the passing years. ~ Audrey Hepburn

Chapter Seven
Enjoying Your Kids to the Fullest by Developing Wonderful Behavior

Mommy's Dilemma

One day as my husband came home from work Lucy greeted her daddy at the door with a big hug. She was *so* excited to see Daddy. Mommy and Daddy started talking about their days and comparing notes and soon Lucy started to feel ignored. She walked over to her baby brother and smacked him, then looked back at us with an evil grin. Daddy warned, "You better stop hitting your brother!"

Then Lucy walked over to the couch and stood up on it and started jumping. She was grinning at her daddy, daring us to yell at her. Daddy didn't say anything because he was tired and had just come home from a long day at work. I didn't say anything because I wanted everyone to get along and I didn't want to interfere with the daddy/daughter relationship.

A few minutes later, she ran up and smacked her baby brother. Again. "Stop that," my husband said. "Don't you know you're not supposed to hit people?"

Then my husband looked at me, as if to say, "Why are you letting her do this? Why can't she just be nice when I get home from work?"

Again, I swept everything under the rug. Obviously, she just needed more attention and I knew things would settle down after a few minutes. The only problem was that they didn't settle down and things continued to get worse until everyone was at each other's throats and the night was ruined.

We struggled with this scenario every night for months. It was putting a strain on our marriage because I didn't know what to do with our daughter, but I knew that I wanted Daddy and daughter to get along better. Clearly, she needed more attention, but I also began to face the fact that she was turning bratty. I often threatened timeout, but I hated to put her in timeout all day long, so my threats were often empty. Daddy tried to be tough with her, but that meant he was yelling at her all the time and it was beginning to really damage their relationship. The truth was, neither of us enjoyed being home with our kids during this period.

We needed help. We consulted a few experts and were told that Lucy's behavior issues were probably related to two things: needing *better* discipline and more challenging activities. We came up with a plan and within a few months, Lucy was a different kid. Her Daddy suddenly *loved* coming home from work and she followed him around obediently when he was home. Suddenly life was fun again.

Teacher's Advice

Life isn't fun when your child is constantly in trouble and is on the verge of a breakdown. Lucy is not unique. We have all seen children at the store or the mall who are clearly out of control and Mom and Dad simply don't know what to do. If your child is like Lucy and is past age two and you still find yourself on constant pins and needles, your child probably needs at least one of three things:

1. More challenging activities
2. More sleep
3. More discipline

More Challenging Activities

When Katie first started having trouble with Lucy, she discovered that her daughter was not being challenged enough throughout the day. Part of the plan was to introduce some fine motor and sensory activities. Katie was amazed by the drastic change in Lucy. Children really do need time to explore and learn. This also boosts self-esteem and confidence as well as fosters the relationship between child and parent. If your child spends most of his or her day being in trouble, consider implementing some of the following:

- Sensory activities (Chapter One)
- Fine Motor Skills (Chapter Two)
- Craft and Art Projects (Chapter Three)

More Sleep

Marc Weissbluth, M.D., wrote an outstanding book on sleep, called *Healthy Sleep Habits, Healthy Child*. In this book, Dr. Weissbluth addresses the importance of sleep for young children: "Evidence that social learning, temperament and sleep habits go together comes from my nap study. Among the children I studied were three between the ages of two and three who stopped napping....and when they stopped napping they underwent what looked like a personality transplant! Fatigue masked their sweet temperaments."

If your child won't stay in bed, consider reading a book about sleep. Children crave routines and consistency. Tell your child what you expect for their bedtime routine and stick to it. Consider investing in a "Tot Alarm Clock." You can program the clock to be blue during a set period of sleep time, then it will turn yellow when that time is up. The night and nap durations are configurable. This also works for the morning wake-up time. You can set it to turn yellow after a certain time, hopefully, after 7 a.m. for most parents.

Forcing your child to stay in his or her room during nap time isn't mean. This alone time can be very beneficial for both parents *and* for the child. It helps them learn to play alone, become more independent, and encourages imaginary play. Baby monitors allow you to listen to what is happening in their room, if you need more comfort knowing what they are doing. Of course, a screaming child may need to be comforted. Make sure they are not ill or scared but don't be manipulated.

Sticker reward charts work well for some children. Determine a specific number of stickers they need to earn before they are rewarded with something special. Then tell them they only get a sticker if they stay in their room quietly during nap time and nighttime. Then, when they reach the goal, make a HUGE deal out of it. Jump around the room and congratulate them and then give them a few pieces of their favorite candy or some other immediate reward. This game can go on indefinitely, as long as you keep giving them the reward they like every time they reach their goal. The trick is to keep them interested in the "something special."

More Discipline

If you wonder whether your child really needs more discipline, pause for a minute and consider their behavior. Do they insist that you buy them a toy from every store that you visit and throw a fit if you don't? Does your child ever hit you? Do they protest furiously when you try to make them get into a car seat, sit at the kitchen table, or go to bed? Is your child ever rude and nasty to you or to strangers? Does your child share well with friends?

If your child is causing problems in the household, don't let it slide. Take control and make a change for the better. Mom and Dad need to be on the same page when it comes to parenting and being consistent with rules. Discuss and agree on rules and consequences before incidents happen and work as partners for the good of the family.

Preventing Inappropriate Behavior

It is possible to actually prevent poor behavior. This takes a plan, dedication, and hard work by parents. Observe children and anticipate problems before they escalate. Young children need to be supervised. Sometimes ignoring misbehavior is the best solution. Perhaps an unhappy look from you is all that is necessary. Warn children of transitions such as the end of play time, going to another location, or that nap or bedtime is nearing. Use your voice, hands, facial expressions, and actions as tools to maintain control and to prevent problems. When things are going well, your voice can be soft, natural, and casual. When you sense a need for more control, your voice can be firm and say, "Take it easy now. Slow down." Borrow the Teacher Stance: One hand on your hip and the other hand waving your pointy finger, face in a frown.

It is also important to teach children to use words instead of force: "*Tell* her what you want. *Think* about what you are doing. *Be careful.* We don't want anyone to get hurt."

Although it's tempting, try to limit the time children spend in front of electronic gadgets. Real back-and-forth communication and interaction is necessary for growth in vocabulary, expression, comprehension, and social skills. Pre-approve television viewing or check electronic games for violence, disrespectful attitudes, or words and actions that you do not want your child to imitate.

Young children need action. They need time for hard physical play to release stress, learn social skills, develop motor skills and to just be a kid. Children need activities that are appropriate for their age and abilities. The goal is for children to accomplish what *they* can do. Above all, treat children with unconditional love. It is the behavior that is unacceptable—the child is loved no matter what.

Giving Children Choices to Prevent Misbehavior

Another way to prevent misbehavior is to give children choices whenever possible. They enjoy feeling that they are in control of their little lives. Here is a scenario of what not to do:

"Come here, honey. It's time to do your hair."

The child yells, "NOOO!" and runs away. Then Mommy tries to tackle her daughter and pin her down as the darling daughter squirms and screams the whole time. Mommy threatens discipline, but never follows through with it. Both are worn out and the hair is still not brushed.

Here are words that work to everyone's benefit: "Honey, would you like your hair in pigtails or a ponytail today?"

Now the child is able to participate in the decision-making process and choose pigtails OR a ponytail. Children thrive on having choices and some control over their day. This works for many things: "Would you like to put on your pants or shirt first?" or "Would you like to wear your sandals or tennis shoes?"

The trick is that you're not giving them a choice of whether or not to do it. You are making it inevitable that it will happen, but you are giving your child a choice of *how* it will happen. Some parents say, "My child won't decide. They just never respond, so this doesn't work for me."

In that case, you decide for them. "Pigtails it is." They'll learn quickly that they need to decide. Once children feel the power of having choices in their lives, they tend to behave better and be more confident.

Shaping Positive Behavior and Increasing Self-Esteem

One of the best ways to make your home more peaceful to is to make sure that your child has high self-esteem. You as a parent truly do have the ability to shape positive behavior.

1. **Praise your child's strengths** making them feel special, important and wanted. Every day, compliment them, give them a hug and tell them you love them. The most precious words will then be heard by you, "I wuuvv you, too."

2. **Focus for 15 minutes a day per child of interrupted one-on-one time**. Great results may be seen with only 15 minutes of uninterrupted concentration on a child. Then they may have the desire and confidence to work/play/learn on their own giving you some downtime. Turn off the phone, or put it on silent, so that it won't be disruptive to your child's special time. Adults can usually wait awhile for your phone or email response.

3. **Help your child develop problem-solving and decision-making skills**. Let them get their own drink or snacks by putting them in reachable places so they can learn some independence skills. Common sense is needed, but children are capable of accomplishing many tasks with encouragement, patience, and praise. Talk about solutions to problems. If you don't know the answer to one of their numerous questions, tell them: "I don't know. Let's find out together."

4. **Stay positive with your child**. Don't compare them to others. Every child is different with their

own strengths and personality. Focus on what they *can* do and provide challenges and opportunities that are appropriate for their level of development. Your child's sense of value is directly related to how you treat them and respond to their accomplishments. Family members are the most important people in the world to little ones.

5. **Provide reasonable choices** for your child such as, "Would you like to have oatmeal or eggs for breakfast?" If you are staying home, let them choose what to wear and make as many choices as is reasonable.

6. **Provide opportunities for your child to help and praise them frequently**. Use a sticker chart or draw happy faces on the calendar when your child has wonderful behavior or learns something new. Treat them to something special when the stickers or happy faces have accumulated to a pre-determined number. The best rewards cost little—except your time. Counting the stickers will reinforce math also. Or fill up a Marble Jar. Use a clear jar and put marbles, rocks, Pom-poms or cotton balls in the jar when good behavior occurs. When the jar if full, give your child a pre-established reward. Let them help decide what the reward will be. Remember, trips to the library and park are free, educational, social, and healthy.

7. **Help your child make a book, box or sack titled *I Like Me!*** Include their letter scribbles, drawings and photos. Print their words on the front or back showing your child that letters have meaning. Read the notes and book on days when you wonder: *Who's child is this? What was I thinking?*

Books to Promote Self-Esteem

- *Guess How Much I Love You* by Sam McBratney
- *I Like Me* by Nancy L. Carlson
- *I Like Myself* by Karen Beaumont
- *Love You Forever* by Robert Munsch
- *I Love You Always and Forever* by Jonathan Emmett
- *How Do I Love* You by P. K. Hallinan
- *I Know Who I Am* by P. K. Hallinan
- *I Know I Belong* by P. K. Hallinan
- *The Kissing Hand* by Audrey Penn

Letting Children Experience the Effect of their Inappropriate Behavior

Even when you try to prevent inappropriate behavior, children will still make the wrong choices occasionally. When this happens, every action should cause a reaction. Take away privileges when inappropriate or disruptive behavior occurs and fewer unwanted episodes will occur. Withdrawing privileges is a behavior shaper where you will always have plenty of options. Temporarily take away what they enjoy doing or a toy they cherish. Losing privileges will work if it is part of a pre-agreed behavior management strategy. In other words, make the rules and state the consequences before episodes occur. Do not feel guilty about enforcing a consequence. The child made the wrong choice. You may want to use empathy such as acknowledging that you realize the child has had an important privilege taken away. But the next time he or she will know that you mean what you say and this should help prevent future problems and confrontations.

If we shelter children from consequences and distort true cause and effect, children rarely become accountable. Instead, they become confused and go through life blaming someone else for their misfortune and "bad luck." Enforced consequences motivate children to develop self control. Learning self control, and how to interact respectfully with others, supports children's self esteem and benefits society in general.

Discipline needs to be consistent, fair and non-emotional. Don't yell. Just decide in advance what the punishment will be, communicate that with your child, and follow through—every time.

For example, if your child has a habit of hitting her sibling, let her know that if she keeps using her doll to hit her brother, she isn't going to get to play with that doll anymore. Then, the next time she hits, walk calmly to her, collect the doll from your child and calmly place the doll on top of the fridge so that it's out of reach. Your child will be distraught, but she has learned that her behavior has real, unpleasant consequences instead of emotional, empty threats. After several minutes, allow her to "earn" the doll back. She can clean the windows or pick up her toys. She must do something actionable to earn the doll back. After she is finished, she gets her doll back.

See how this works? She doesn't want to hit brother anymore because now she loses her doll and also has to clean the windows. Don't get mad or say things you will regret later. A child's self-esteem is left intact because Mom didn't yell or hit and also because the child accomplished a task.

Young children are not experienced enough, or emotionally mature enough, to be in charge of themselves. They need guidance, direction, time, patience and dedicated parents who set firm rules and stick to them. Parents need to be good role models using consistent discipline with rewards and consequences. Children should be expected to obey adults–provided the adults are reasonable. But young children need time and help to understand established boundaries, rules, and consequences of their behavior.

Consistency, routines, and stability at home will reinforce good behavior and increase a child's sense of security and self-esteem. Your children will imitate you because they live with you and they love you. Parenting is a huge responsibility but it becomes easier the more you establish love, trust, stability and discipline. Be a model of good behavior to help them grow into respectful, happy, creative, contributing members of society.

Poor Behavior—What to Do

We've all witnessed a child throwing a temper tantrum: Screaming, hitting, biting, trying to escape, or sobbing uncontrollably because they did not get their way. They are angry and frustrated. As their anger increases, it becomes more difficult for an adult to remain in control. But the adult must remember that this is a young child who does not have the life experiences of an adult.

The adult must state the rules—which should already have been established. "I cannot let you hit or hurt others." Kneel down and talk to the child directly while looking into their eyes, holding the child if necessary. Do not waste your breath talking, scolding, or explaining when children are not really listening. Lead the child to an appropriate setting. If your child throws a temper tantrum in a store, lead them out of the store or hold them until they gain control. Remain calm but firm and in control.

Use your arms to hold the child. Children will benefit by your control and your understanding, and will be all right. The child will remember that you are not the enemy and that you have ways to help them establish self-control. When you hold, rather than hit, you are protecting as well as controlling a child. Some children do not want to be held, but would prefer letting off steam by hitting a pillow.

Try and understand *why* the child is behaving inappropriately as you settle them down. Are they tired, hungry, scared, excited, had too much sugar, or are they experiencing instability? When they are ready to listen, speak to the child kindly, but with authority and direction about how they should behave.

Demonstrate how to behave. You have to show children *how to act,* not how *not* to act.

Keep your emotions under control. Here are some ways:
1. Take a deep breath, hold it, let it out. Repeat this several times as your body relaxes.
2. Encourage your child to do deep breathing along with you.
3. Say a mantra inside your head: "I'm the adult. I'm the role model. I'm in control."
4. Focus on staying in control and on being an example of good behavior.
5. Count to 10. This saying has been around a long time. It must work.
6. Think about why the child is acting this way. If you don't know, try and find out when the episode has subsided. Knowing the reason may give you those extra seconds of patience that is needed before you lose it too.

Do not slap or spank a child. When adults hit children to get them to mind, too much has already gone wrong and the discipline has broken down. We know a big person should not hit a smaller person. Adults must set the example for good behavior. Therefore, you do not spit when you want a child to stop spitting, you do not yell when you want a child to stop yelling, and you do not hit when you want a child to stop hitting. Years of emotional scarring and damage can result when a child is mistreated by an adult, whether verbally or physically.

Consequences—The Good, the Bad and the Ugly

Consequences do not need to be dehumanizing, demeaning, humiliating, or full of nagging and scolding. Three questions to ask when delivering a consequence are:

1. Is it justified?
2. Is it respectful?
3. Is it reasonable?

Thinking about this quote by Glennon Melton by help you put behavior incidents into perspective: "Don't let yourself become so concerned with raising a good kid that you forget you already have one."

Phrase Tips:

"No means *no*. I don't argue with children. I'm the adult." The more this is repeated, the better it works. You can use empathy, but stick to your plan. Perhaps the child is mature enough to understand the reasons why you have said *no* such as weather, money, time, or health concerns. Regardless, they need to know that you mean what you say. If your child has opportunities for many fun, educational, interesting, and engaging activities, they will have fewer behavior problems. Remember this phrase too: Every day, tell your child that you love them and you will hear the most precious words in the world, "I wuv you too, Mom."

A child needs your love more, when he deserves it least. ~Erma Bombeck

Part II: School Readiness for Kindergarten

Chapter Eight
How to Prepare Your Child for Kindergarten

Mommy's Dilemma

I've never considered myself to be someone who coddles my children. From the start I wasn't afraid of timeouts or enforcing bedtime. I read somewhere that just because a child will cry when you pull them away from the fire doesn't mean you shouldn't pull them away. Yes, it upsets them, but, of course, it is best for them.

Despite this attitude, I tend to do everything for my children. I put on my daughter's shoes, wipe her when she goes potty, and open all her snacks for her. We're often in a hurry to get out the door so it just makes sense for me to do it. It's faster.

Yet, one day Lucy had a friend over. The girls were exactly the same age and when it was time for her to go, I offered to help the little girl put her shoes on. She looked at me like I had two heads.

"I can put on my own shoes," she told me.

Lucy told me after her friend left, "Taylor went potty—all by herself." I was a little shocked, but also impressed. Every time Lucy needed to potty she announced it to the world, expecting me to watch her, praise her, and wipe her. And I obliged every time without thinking much about it. It just seemed natural. Yet, here was a little girl the exact same age, doing all these things by herself.

After Lucy's friend left, I started thinking about this. It never occurred to me to expect Lucy to put on her own shoes. At age three-and-a-half, I still knelt down in front of her every day and I even patted myself on the back because she knew left and right. Isn't that enough to expect of a three year old? Yet apparently, other kids were doing these things. So, why wasn't Lucy?

I suddenly had visions of Lucy going to Kindergarten and being the only one still asking the teacher to put her shoes on and even worse—to wipe her after using the potty. She would be ostracized! Maybe even laughed at!

I decided I needed to nip this in the bud right then and there. I explained the situation to the babysitter so she could get on board. She looked a little confused, paused for a second, and said, "Well, actually Lucy has been wiping herself and putting on her own shoes for months now. Doesn't she do that for you?"

Well, you would think that I would know my own daughter, but apparently I was wrong! At that point, I realized that I needed to adjust my own behavior if I was going to prepare her for Kindergarten.

Teacher's Advice

It is understandable that Katie was still helping Lucy put on her shoes and with potty needs. Lucy is her first child and Katie has a strong desire to be a wonderful mother. Each child is different, but it is perfectly natural to compare our children with other children, thereby learning what your child may perhaps be able to do at a certain age and time.

Young children change and grow at an amazing rate. What they cannot do one month, will come much easier a few months later. Children are eager to learn and to please their parents and a little encouragement goes a long way. Velcro is one of the greatest inventions ever made for parents. Buy shoes with Velcro and praise your child for putting on their shoes and strapping them by themselves. Tying shoes with laces is very difficult, requiring several fine motor steps, and is usually not mastered until a child is five or six. As for using the potty, cleanliness is important for health and hygiene reasons, so moms may want to make sure their child is clean and washes their hands after they use the bathroom. Independence is craved by most children, so let them be as independent as is reasonable.

How to Help Your Child Prepare for School

Children are excited about starting school, yet also a little afraid. Starting school means changes in their daily routine including being away from home, learning new rules and following directions from other adults. There are many opportunities for parents to foster school readiness, thereby reducing the amount of stress experienced by children and by parents. It is natural to have doubts and fears about change. Talk to your child about what they can expect. This will help you both feel more secure. Encourage independence in your child. As we saw in Katie's example, children are often capable of far more than we realize. Stretch their boundaries. Encourage and reward them when they attempt to do things for themselves.

In addition to talking to children about general feelings of starting school, it is also helpful to make sure they are ready from an academic standpoint. Of course, we send children to Kindergarten expecting they will learn many things, but the more they know going in, the easier the transition will be for everyone, including the teacher.

The good news is that the most important way you can help your child learn is through playing with them! There is ample research supporting that the way young children learn is through playful, age appropriate, readiness activities rather than screen time or flashcards. Providing ample playtime is the way your child will be ready to learn academics when they reach Kindergarten. The tide is being turned from testing preschoolers and pushing them to learn specific skills, to letting them learn naturally, exploring, testing, manipulating their environment while learning, developing problem-solving skills, and making sense of their rapidly changing world. The whole child needs to be developed through social, cognitive, physical, emotional and language rich experiences.

You may wonder: Why is my child repeating the same kind of tasks over and over? Why are they fascinated with rocks, placing them in circles, placing something beside each rock that is lined up? Why do they want the same book read so many times? Why should I play the same game again and again? Some Moms may even worry that their children are autistic, but more likely your child is learning naturally in the following areas: math (one-on-one correspondence of objects, counting, sorting), reading (repetition, rhythm and rhyme), playing peek-a-boo and Hide-and-Seek (object permanence), tossing same object over and over (gravity, cause and effect), spending hours building and manipulating blocks and containers (problem solving skills, math, geometry, engineering), playing with dolls and action figures (fantasy, pretend or imaginative play, creativity, sharing and social skills).

Developmental Areas

Preschoolers are willing and eager to grow and learn. With your help, they will learn at an amazing rate. The following are developmental areas of growth:

1. **Cognitive**: Thinking, expressing, asking questions, following directions, creating things such as in art and block designs.

2. **Social**: Sharing, good sportsmanship, taking turns, forming friendships, language development.
3. **Emotional**: Bonding, feelings of self-worth, confidence in learning new things, can be separated from parents for increasing periods.
4. **Academic**: The names and sounds of letters, number recognition and concept, interested in learning on own.
5. **Physical**: Development of gross motor skills, followed by fine motor skills (Discussed in Chapters Two, Four and Five.)

Cognitive Preparation

Communication

Decode your child's questions. A curious child's questions may seem never ending but they reflect their cognitive and emotional development. Parents should take those questions seriously and answer them in a way that will strengthen and deepen the relationship. Stop what you are doing and listen to what they are asking. You don't always have to say "yes" to their requests. Say yes only when it is in the child's best interest. Be objective and help children take responsibility for their behavior. When you need to say "no," give a reason or use empathy. "I know you want to play outside, but it is dark now. We'll play outside another time when it is daylight."

Talk to your child as you perform chores. Questions that begin with *who, what, when, where* or *why* can encourage your child to talk and think. Help your child develop thinking skills such as being able to pay attention and follow simple instructions. Gradually, increase the steps in following instructions. "Get your shoes and put them on, please." "Go to the bathroom, flush the toilet, and wash your hands, please."

Teach your child to say their first and last name clearly and loudly (the cafeteria cashier needs this information). Have your child make friends with neighborhood children. Preschool or Mother's Day Out help prepare children for Kindergarten, but never underestimate the time a parent and child spend together.

Encourage Independence in Your Child

- Encourage your child to try new things. Compliment them when they do.
- Give your child time to answer questions.
- Child-proof your home to encourage more freedom.
- Try not to do things for your child that they can do for themselves, such as getting a drink or snack or dressing themselves.
- Shelves and toy boxes should be easily accessible so children can put away their books, toys and clothes.

Social Preparation

Good manners and Good choices

Say "please" and "thank you" often and your child will too. Explain that good manners help people get along with each other and make friends. Teach your child how to listen without interrupting.

Explain why sharing toys with others is important. Sharing helps everyone have more fun. Play a card or board game that involves taking turns. Demonstrate good sportsmanship.

Ask children to pick up toys at the end of play. Thank them for helping. Praise, compliment and reward your child when you see him sharing toys, cleaning or helping others. Rewards can be smiles and hugs or saying, "You are so wonderful to help with cleaning. Thank you for being kind and helpful."

Use words to talk about feelings such as being happy, sad, excited, worried, scared, curious or hurt. Help your children use words, not force, when they are angry. Communicate your thoughts and feelings to your child and have conversations. Explain that children are expected to raise their hand when they want to ask the teacher a question at school.

Let your child make choices between two good choices, such as what clothing to wear, book to read, or game to play. Choose clothes that are comfortable and easy for toileting. Making choices builds independence and self-confidence forming an "I can do it" attitude. Compliment children on the skills they have already accomplished.

Emotional Preparation

Self-esteem is the confidence and satisfaction children have in themselves. In psychology, self-esteem reflects a person's overall self-worth. The development of a positive self concept is extremely important to the overall well-being of a child and to reaching their potential. Parents are instrumental in building self-esteem in their children. The following are indicators of a healthy self-esteem:

- Able to take reasonable risks
- Feels worthwhile and lovable
- Makes friends easily
- Displays positive attitudes to others most of the time
- Generally behaves well and is able to control behavior
- Enjoys learning new activities showing enthusiasm
- Can accept they are going to make mistakes and experience failure
- Likes to be creative and have their own ideas

- Can be cooperative and follow age-appropriate rules
- Generally willing to try new things and can show initiative as opposed to children with low self-esteem who give up easily or show little confidence in areas that are new
- Acknowledges their own contributions to success
- Usually optimistic and uses positive language

Parenting Skills to Help Preschoolers

Give full attention to child: Turn off the television, put down the phone and listen when your child speaks. Give them time to finish a thought or ask a question. Make eye contact unless you are driving. The timing of their important questions won't always be convenient. Most experts agree that the most "teachable" moments are spontaneous, casual opportunities.

Make available one-on-one time: It is natural for siblings to be jealous of parent time. Each child needs opportunities to be the focus of attention, with a parent listening and answering their questions and spending time doing something they enjoy. This is a great time to promote self-esteem. When possible, let your child decide what you will do with your together time.

Be honest: Your answer may be "I don't know; let's find out together." Reminding children that grown-ups don't know everything and have to figure things out too gives children key problem-solving skills and permission to make mistakes. Having a sense of humor about our own shortcomings also relieves tension and provides a great way to laugh with our children.

Encourage and respect children's opinions and feelings: Try to remember that children perceive problems and conflicts differently. They do not have the years of experience that we have and more importantly, they lack the verbal skills to express emotions. Encourage and model for your child how to express feelings; for example, "I need to make sure I understand. You're sad/mad because..." Or, "You seem really upset. Can you tell me why?" Repeating, identifying emotions, and clarifying questions invite children to speak up and to consider the impact of their words and feelings on others.

Routine, Ritual, Ready-to-Read Time

People do better with a routine. Children crave stability, consistency and even boundaries, which promotes security and a feeling of safety. Devise a ritual of reading together in the same place at the same time. Bedtime is best because it leaves your child feeling loved before sleeping. Even parents will benefit from this reading ritual. Take a deep breath and be with your child in the moment. Put other thoughts and worries aside. Enjoy this special time.

Experts recommend reading three books together each night or five a day. Don't read any if you, or your child, are too tired, or ill, because it can become a power struggle. But every night, when possible, read with your child. Three categories of books to read are: a book for learning about animals or science, a book of rhyming, and a book of the child's choice even if you do most, or all, of the reading. A child may choose the same book over and over. Read it again and again. Memorization is one of the beginning stages of reading. Repetition instills security in a child; a much needed treasure in our fast-paced world.

Academic Preparation

Perhaps your child has mastered the following skills in pre-Kindergarten, but it is important for parents to be a part of a child's learning and to encourage them through open-ended exploration, providing ample opportunities for growth and expanding and extending learning. These skills will help your child be ready for Kindergarten:

- Count to 10
- Recognize groups of one through five
- Recognize circle, square, triangle
- Trace basic shapes
- Sort objects by color, size and shape
- Cut with scissors
- Recognize rhyming sounds
- Manage bathroom needs
- Button and zip clothes
- Put shoes on and take shoes off
- Share with others
- Listen without interrupting
- Follow simple directions
- Demonstrate self-control
- Separate from parents without being upset
- Speak understandably in sentences of five words
- Identify some alphabet letters
- Identify sounds of some letters and words
- Recognize some sight words like "stop"
- Bounce a ball, jump, climb, hop, skip

Brain Development

Research has revealed that the early years of life are critical to a child's brain development. Children's brains are only 25 percent developed at birth. From that moment, whenever a baby is fed, cuddled, played with, talked to, sung to, or read to, the other 75 percent of its brain begins to develop. The more stimulation the baby has through its senses of touch, taste, smell, sight and sound, the more rapidly that development will occur. Children need to have loving, laughing, deep and meaningful conversations with adults. They may not be able to answer you back, but they are absorbing and learning much more than they are capable of expressing. Many experts believe that a child's IQ development is a reflection of their preschool agenda.

Developmental Psychologist Gordon Neufeld is the author of *Hold On To Your Kids: Why Parents Need to Matter More Than Peers*, and is a widely respected therapist and author. Neufeld believes that: "Play—not achieving academic results—should be at the center of early childhood education." Children will learn academics at school but the preschool years are the time to build a strong foundation in a nurturing family where a child can feel unconditional love, thereby giving them the confidence and desire to learn more. Neufeld believes the early years are the time for a child to form a strong attachment to their parents and that this is much more important than forming attachments to peers, or being rushed from one activity to another.

Neufeld states: "Play helps children build problem-solving networks. At four, five, even six, children are not ready to learn by working because the prefrontal cortex, the part of the brain where a child is capable of mixed feelings, is still under construction. It only gets wired between five and seven years of age." Neufeld further states: "Play helps children build problem-solving networks. But that's only if the play is expressive and doesn't have any consequences for making mistakes, or have expected outcomes."

Education officials counter by saying that play should be a central part of preschoolers' learning, but that kids also need to be ready to learn when they start school.

That is true. But, according to many child development theorists, providing ample playtime is the way to get there. Childhood play is crucial for social, emotional and cognitive development and for parental attachment. Your child will learn academics in Kindergarten. Of course, provide opportunities for children to learn numbers and letters—through sensory/motor integration, using their five senses, and teaching by linking to what is relevant and interesting in their world. But know when to back off if the child loses interest, their eyes glaze over, they become frustrated or anxious, or it is harming their self-esteem. The public school curriculum mandates specific skills be taught and tested—whether your child has mastered them, or not. So now is the time to PLAY, BOND, AND ENJOY YOUR CHILD'S CHILDHOOD WITH THEM.

I think, at a child's birth, if a mother could ask a fairy godmother to endow it with the most useful gift, that gift should be curiosity. ~ Eleanor Roosevelt

Chapter Nine
Helping Your Child Learn to Read

Mommy's Dilemma

After I had my first baby, I quickly realized that life was all about milestones. Strangers and family alike were constantly asking things like:

"Has she rolled over yet?"

"Is she walking yet?"

"I bet she's talking a lot, right?"

The problem is that if your little one *isn't* doing something, you feel ashamed and worried that she is behind. When Lucy was about three, I began to feel the pressure to teach her the letters of the alphabet. My friends would tell me how their child knew every letter in the alphabet already. Although I tried to encourage her interest, she just wasn't. Since I didn't know anything about teaching, I started with what seemed logical to me—I bought some flashcards with letters and pictures. I gave it a valiant effort, but I was finally forced to admit that she wasn't even remotely interested in flashcards, even if they had pictures of cows and cats. I gave up for several months, but then started to feel the pressure again.

I decided I needed a new tactic. This time I bought a cool easel with colorful magnetic letters. I placed the letters to her name in a row on the easel and became very excited when she would point to the "L" as I said the letter.

Again, she was interested for about two minutes but then ran away from me. I was left wondering what I could possibly do to entice her to learn letters. Not only was she not interested, but I was beginning to be concerned that she might be dyslexic. Every time we tried to encourage her to write letters, she printed them backwards—and she didn't even notice that they were backwards. She would write what looked like a 3 and proudly yell, "E!"

My husband and I were starting to worry. Finally, I tried something that really worked. For this project, our materials were simple—white glue, construction paper, and sprinkles. Some people use glitter, but I read somewhere that you should NEVER use glitter with little kids because it can get on their hands and then if they rub their eyes it can damage their cornea. Instead, I used the leftover green and red sprinkles from making Christmas cookies.

Jacob wasn't quite two at the time, but I knew he would want to participate. So I simply wrote out their names on the paper with glue, then I let them drop the sprinkles to make their name come to life for them. I was utterly amazed at their reaction. They were both intrigued and kept begging me to do more!

They adored pulling the finished product out of the pan to see what they had created.

That's the babysitter's name, Renee. They call her Nene. After we finished, Lucy was so excited to show Nene!

They were sad when I finally ran out of glue, but we put all of the completed names on the kitchen table and I pronounced each name for Lucy so that she could see what she had spelled. I used her friend's and grandparent's names and she was totally intrigued. By the end of this play/work time, she could pick out each name and I even heard her telling Jacob, "See? This spells Paaapppaaaa. Don't worry, Jacob, one day you'll be able to read like me."

Teacher's Advice

A Cautionary Note: Please do not stress yourself or your young child if they are not reading before they enter school. Jean Piaget, respected theorist on the stages of child development, believed:

1. Not all children are ready to read at the same age and in the same manner,
2. Not all children are ready to read before first grade,
3. Not all children learn in the same manner, and
4. Reading is a great deal more than decoding printed symbols on a page and mouthing words.

William Crain's wrote in his book *Theories of Development* the following about young children learning from a computer screen but I think it also explains why children are not attracted to flashcards: "The computer monitor presents only symbols—words, pictures, numbers and graphs. The child is exposed to a great deal of information, but the child receives it on a purely secondhand, mental level. The child learns symbols, but without the personal, bodily, sensory experiences that make the symbols meaningful. The danger is that the child who is learning a great deal for the first time at the computer terminal is learning at too cerebral a level. The child is becoming a disembodied mind."

The most important thing a parent can do for a child is to love them, fostering their self-esteem and encouraging their natural love of learning. A parent's responsibility is to provide meaningful opportunities for growth, respecting children as individuals capable of learning at their own pace, in their own time and in their own way. But there are simple ways to help your child learn reading skills.

Letters and Words are Everywhere

Parents can help their children learn to read by observing environmental print. Letters and words are on transportation signs, buses, stores, billboards, newspaper comics, game instructions, grocery lists, menus, and food containers to name a few. Point and say letters, numbers, shapes and words around the house and when you take a walk or a drive. You will be surprised what children will remember the next time you pass a favorite sign or billboard. A child's favorite word is their name. Find the letters in their first name in other places.

Run your finger under words and say the label before giving your child something from a game box or food container. This will help them learn that reading is from left to right and from top to bottom.

Most importantly, let your child see that you enjoy reading and writing. Take children's books with you for those slow times at the doctor's office. You will have fewer behavior problems if your child is actively engaged. Also, keep children's books in the car along with crayons and tablets. If you don't want melted crayons in your car, let your child use colored pencils.

How many parents have sighed as their children scream at a McDonald's golden arch? That arch symbol means food and fun. Many children can "read" store signs. They may point and scream, "W-a-l-m-a-r-t! That spells *groceries!*" They are making the symbol/letter/reading connection. Your reminders will encourage children to grasp the connection. Compliment children often for their accomplishments. It's a big world, after all.

The Reading /Writing Connection

The reading/writing connection is essential and speeds up the process of reading. Let your child see you writing. This art is being left unseen with the onset of computers. Give meaning to your writing for the child to witness, and participate in, whenever possible. When your child is interested, help them print, copy, or trace a grocery list or a list of errands. Let them cross off the list as it is accomplished. This gives meaning to the written word. Let children check a chore chart earning a reward when a certain number of checks are reached. Help them write the date on the chart. If they witness you writing events on a calendar, they will link the reading/writing connection as the events happen such as birthdays, doctor visits, library books due, and visits from relatives or friends.

Help your child print a list of things to do or chores, a note to dad, a letter to grandmother, or a thank you note to someone. Thank you notes are greatly appreciated even if your child only signs his or her name. Perhaps you could write a simple note letting them trace the letters or write a note that they can copy to another piece of paper. A simple "Thank you. Love, name" may be treasured, especially with a drawing. It shows that some time and thought was given to that person.

Parent/Child Reading Time

It is never too early to begin reading to your child. Some parents read to their baby while he/she is in the womb. We've all heard of musical prodigies whose parents played Mozart for a lift in IQ before the baby was born, revealing that neuron connections are being formed before birth. Research shows that infants recognize their mother's voice and are attracted to it. They have been listening to her voice for nine months before birth.

With your baby sitting on your lap, begin reading and feeling material books that can be washed. Inexpensive material books can be purchased which have interesting flaps or gadgets attached. Look for thick hard books that have different textures for a child to feel and associate with a word.

After your child starts talking, find a picture book without words. Ask your child to tell you the story based on what they see. This builds thinking and comprehension skills. Or ask your child to tell you the story using their own words from books you have read to them. Did they understand the book? Can they tell you what happened? Who was their favorite character? How did the book make them feel? Was it funny or amazing? Why do they like it? Find other books of similar interest at the library to create a desire for them to learn to read. Learning to read happens with baby steps and opportunities.

Start a Conversation about a Book

Mom: "What book shall we read?"

Child: "The dinosaur book!"

Oh goodie, I've already read that until it's falling apart. "Why do you like this book?"

"I like dinosaurs."

"What kind of dinosaurs?"

"Green ones."

"So, the green dinosaur followed his mother one day and they went to the ...?"

"To the park."

"They went to the park and they played on the..."

"They went down the slide!"

Oh my, that must have been a tight squeeze. "They went down the slide. Did they both go down the slide?"

"No, silly. The mom was too fat. She got on the swing."

All righty then, a green dinosaur on a swing. "And then what happened?"

By encouraging your child to tell a story, you are helping them develop vocabulary and comprehension skills as well as their creativity. You will learn a lot about what your child likes by asking *them* questions. Reading the printed word is just a step in reading. It is important for your child to comprehend what the story is about and to understand the vocabulary. That is why real talking back and forth is so essential to growth.

Some experts recommend reading three to five books a day to a child. Don't read any if you or your child are too sick or tired. Then it becomes a power struggle. But every day or night that you can, read and share books with your child. It is the most important time that you can spend to help them develop reading, listening and comprehension skills. They will learn about the world as you take a peek into theirs.

The Three Rs of Reading: Repetition, Rhythm and Rhyme

There are visual learners, auditory learners and sensory/motor/integration learners. Teaching by using all of the five senses creates enthusiastic readers. Children must find a book interesting by textures, sounds, illustrations, or content. Young children enjoy hearing your voice in rhythm and rhyming sounds. Children may want to "read" the book to you. Let them re-tell the book in their own words or from memorization. This is a beginning step to reading.

Your child may show an interest in letters around three, especially if they have an older sibling or watch shows like *Sesame Street*. If you think it is the right time, you could teach some pre-reading skills. If they are not interested, try it again in a few months and you may be surprised at the difference in their interest.

Children enjoy sensory learning such as tracing their name in shaving cream, finger paint, cool whip, and even applesauce. They can form letters with playdough, clay, pretzels, M&Ms, buttons, beads, cereal, pasta, beans, corn, or seeds. You could print out block letters or make them yourself and your child could color the letter or fill it in with objects that begin with that letter. Children enjoy sensory tubs. They could find objects that start with the letter sound and put them in the tub or box. Put an index card on the tub with the letter in both upper and lower case.

Phonics

Phonics is teaching the sounds of the letters. *Sesame Street* on TV or *Koala's ABC Phonics Chant* on *You Tube* lets children hear the correct pronunciation of letter sounds which leaves off vowel sounds after consonants, for example: Bb is pronounced b not beeee or baaaaa.

Reading is accomplished by slowly blending letter sounds. Put your finger under each letter of a word making its sound. Stretch out sounds then gradually blend the sounds together at a faster pace. Like: ccc aaaaaaaa ttt as you run your finger under the word *cat*. Then put the sounds together: cat. Your child could move a car or train slowly then increase in speed as you blend the sounds faster.

Learning letters and phonics through movement and action helps children learn. Play Blue's Clues and ask questions to help lead to objects that begin with that sound. Start with the letters in your child's name. For example, if your child's name is Ben, begin with the letter B. Have a big box and label it Bb.

- Toss Bb objects into box: beads, beans, buttons, banana, band-aid, bracelet, blocks, bats, beenie babies, bunny.
- Cut images from magazines to make a B word collage.
- Play and learn about things that begin with B such as boats, balls, bats, butterflies, boxes, birds, bulldozers.
- Do activities such as blowing bubbles, blow paint through a straw, bouncing balloons and balls.
- Take a Scavenger Hunt looking for words with Bb sound.

Memorizing "sight" words is helpful because these common words appear often in print and promote fluency of reading, which increases comprehension. Children who are four and five may be able to learn some sight words if you print them on an index card and practice them. But real life playful learning is much more interesting to a child.

Never force a child to learn something they are not ready to learn or make them feel bad for not learning something that you think is important. This book is for preschool children and they enjoy learning by using their senses and through playful activities. Of course, if they are interested, they may learn to read before entering Kindergarten and that is wonderful, but not required. The teacher will still spend hours on letters and phonics. Now is the time for them to enjoy childhood, build up their self-confidence, and learn about things that are interesting to them, fostering their natural curiosity and innate love of learning.

Teach Your Child How to Print their First Name

What is your child's favorite word? Their name! Help them learn how to print it with only the first letter capitalized. Their teachers will appreciate it and this will help your child with reading skills because print is mostly in lower case. Many experts want the child to learn to print the upper case letters before lower case because they are easier to form. But I think an exception can be made for a child's first name so that they don't have to relearn it at the first grade teacher's insistence.

Children of this age are tactile learners meaning they like to touch and feel to explore their world or use their five senses. Here are some ways to help your child learn to print their name:

- Form letters with pretzels, cereal, rocks, pasta, buttons, popcorn, or whatever they like. Encourage your child to move their fingers over the letters. Make it fun and praise often.

- Lightly print your child's name and have them trace it in rainbow colors using different crayon colors over the letters. Or make dots forming the letters and guide them to connect the dots. Make the beginning dot darker or bigger. Encourage children to start at the top and go down. Be patient because letters are formed going left to right *and* going right to left. Children love markers, especially scented ones and this may extend time spent tracing letters (make sure you buy washable markers).

- Put shaving cream on a surface. Help your child trace their name in the mixture. They will love to help you clean away those crayons marks and germs, which the shaving cream dissolves.

- Make playdough and let your child roll it into worm or snake shapes. Then help them form the letters for their first name and run their fingers over the letters. Feel the stress release as you roll playdough snakes. Take deep breaths and enjoy being a child again.

It is extremely important that your child observe you enjoying books. Library books are free to borrow. If you read from an electronic device, then have some ebooks available for your children so they understand that you are reading a book. Explore many free children's ebooks via MeMeTales-website and apps (www.memetales.com) which are available to be viewed on computers, tablets and smart phones. Something about everything can be learned from reading.

There are many little ways to enlarge your child's world. Love of books is the best of all. ~ Jackie Kennedy

Chapter Ten
Helping Your Child Learn Math and Science

Mommy's Dilemma

When Lucy was almost two, we had a visit from our "Parents as Teacher's" lady. It is a really neat program where teachers are assigned to come to your house and observe your child and make sure they are developing normally. If there are concerns, the school district will even pay for early therapy. In most cases, everything is fine and they just give parents ideas on educational activities and things to do with kids. When my lady came for the first time, I felt really behind. I didn't come from an education background; I was a business major. She gave me a whole list of things I should be doing with Lucy. I had no idea that kids were supposed to be "sorting" objects. She told me that I should buy some type of sorting bears or sorting cards and that sorting is really important for young children.

It's not that I didn't believe her. It's just that I was swamped and kept meaning to buy the sorting bears and books about feelings and all the other things on the list and I just never got around to it. Then one day we went to a friend's house. This friend did have sorting bears and the kids played together while I chatted with the other mom. We didn't tell them what to do with the bears. In fact, there were lots of other toys I thought would be more interesting to Lucy than those bears. However, we glanced over at the kids a few minutes later and my mouth almost dropped to the floor. In the span of about two minutes, Lucy had created the most elaborate sorting tower I'd ever seen. Granted, I haven't seen a lot of bear sorting towers in my lifetime, but at that point I realized that my advisor had been correct. Kids were born to sort things. She put the yellow bears on the top, then lined the other bears around them in order of color. Not only that, I could tell she was very proud of herself. I went out that day and bought some of those bears.

Teacher's Advice

Children begin sorting objects at an early age, for they are pattern-seekers. According to some researchers, young children spend over 40 percent of their time sorting objects into sets, counting objects, or exploring patterns and forms. You don't have to buy expensive computer games or use explicit mathematical instruction for your child to learn math. They are doing it naturally with relevant objects. Take advantage of teachable moments and extend their learning. Provide materials for them to feel, manipulate, sort and count.

First, they will be interested in the texture, form or movement of an object. Then they may line up a row of cars, eventually putting an object beside each car (matching and one-on-one correspondence). They are learning about more and less; smaller and bigger; and conservation.

You don't need to buy anything special. Play math games with whatever interests your child—dolls, action figures, marbles, cotton balls, or swings at the park. Count trees or signs as you take a walk. A parent's role is to provide opportunities for growth but also to let children expand their learning in their own way. Listen and watch. You will be amazed at how much time children spend enjoying math discovery—which is helping them acquire reading and science skills during the process.

Use questions to help them clarify their ideas and expand their knowledge, rather than quickly providing them with answers. Extend with more questions or with new vocabulary. Your child's explanations and answers will give you insight into what they already know and how they think. Watch and listen carefully and you will see that they are learning a lot about their world.

Sorting

Children are interested in sorting objects at an early age. Sorting leads to patterning, which also helps children, learn to read due to predictability. Provide opportunities for children to group objects by attributes—or by color, shape, size or texture. Use objects that are interesting to a child—perhaps some things picked up on a walk such as sticks, leaves and rocks—or sort leaves by their color or shape.

Sort by Attributes:

- **Color**: beads, buttons, apples, colored paper, Pom-poms, pipe cleaners
- **Shape**: pieces of paper cut into shapes, buttons, pipe cleaners, coins
- **Size**: action figures, blocks, beenie babies, dolls
- **Texture**: feathers, shells, rocks, toys

Children enjoy matching games using cards of their favorite characters or with objects real in their environment which increases their vocabulary. Another way to increase vocabulary is to compare objects such as same/different, few/many, short/long, heavy/light, green/blue.

Sorting Game: What is Different?

- 2 socks/1 book
- 3 apples/1 orange
- 3 red legos/1 green lego

An extension of sorting would be to overlap two Hula Hoops so that you have a center area placing blue objects on the left, red objects on the right, and objects that have blue and red in the middle. These could be labeled red, blue, mixed. This is a beginning algebra and also a computer programming concept.

Matching cards or objects is a form of sorting. The objective is to make sorting, matching, categorizing and organizing a fun hands-on learning experience that is interesting and relevant to the child's world.

Patterning

Give your child simple tasks that involve matching, sorting, or counting objects. Any interesting objects will work such as marbles, rocks, craft sticks, balls, cards, M&Ms, cereal, pasta, coins, shells, beans, yarn, buttons, socks, towels and utensils. Patterning helps children with math, reading and science skills by use of:

- **Prediction**: What comes next?
- **Ordering**: Sequence of pattern
- **Communication and Vocabulary**: Describe and express patterns. What shape, color, texture?
- **Counting**: Create simple to complex patterns— rock/leaf, rock/rock/leaf. How many are in pattern? What comes next?
- **Measurement**: Compare and contrast objects using terms such as *long, heavy, light, shapes, colors*
- **Sensory/Motor Integration**: How does it feel? Which is heavier?
- **Creativity**: Encourage exploration of objects using the five senses
- **Problem Solving Skills**: Thinking linearly, step-by-step manipulation with results and outcome

Play musical instruments in patterns—ring bells, tap sticks, clap hands and stomp feet in patterns. Encourage your child to make up their own body movement patterns and join the fun.

Patterning Builds Vocabulary

- Names of colors
- Names of shapes
- Textures: soft, hard, bumpy, smooth
- Few, more, less
- Inside, outside
- Left, middle, right
- Above, below
- Top, bottom
- Same, different
- Long, short
- Tall, short
- Big, little
- Light, heavy

Block Play

Blocks are a wonderful source for concrete learning. Blocks also engage children in repetitive behavior which enhances learning. Young children will stack and knock down blocks over and over again because of the sensory rewards. The sight of the blocks falling is fun for a young child who is amazed by the effects of gravity. Block play can be rich in parent/child activity and filled with touch, sight, sound, repetition and imagination.

Maria Montessori, a pioneer in early childhood education, emphasized the importance of concrete forms in math education between the ages of three and five. Math manipulatives (objects that can be sorted, patterned, counted) facilitate the abstract thought needed later to compute numbers. Montessori recommended that young children constantly move objects, like blocks and beads, and use their senses while learning because it leads to a later desire to write out a mathematical operation. Repetition is a necessary ritual for learning, according to Montessori.

If you don't have wooden blocks (or other commercially available building objects), you can make your own blocks out of lightweight cardboard boxes such as tissue and cereal boxes; cool whip and yogurt containers; or oatmeal and coffee canisters. For added weight, pack containers with newspaper and tape them shut. To make them even more interesting, add a few beans or some rice for a sound effect. Even if you already have wooden blocks, consider making cardboard boxes with your child and talking about their size and shape, perhaps painting them, and what you would like to build with them.

Learning with Blocks

- Lay out a pattern with two or three blocks and ask, "What comes next?" You can pattern them by color, size, or shape. Recognizing and predicting patterns is an important logic and math skill.

- Encourage your child to make something of their choice. Let them think about it for awhile. If they need encouragement, consider starting a road, house, fort or animal. Praise them for their efforts and ask, "What are you building?" Preschoolers need help expressing themselves and may just repeat your words. If they don't know what to say, help them with words but give them a chance to tell you first. You could read a book, or take a walk, before playing with blocks to help them devise a block building plan.

- Name the different block shapes and point out similar shapes around the room.

- Encourage your child to sort the blocks by size. Use comparison words like big and small.
- Teaching opposites will build vocabulary using words like: big/small, heavy/light, short/tall, up/down, in/out, few/many, under/over.
- To extend block play, use a tape measure, ruler or yardstick and note differences in the sizes of the blocks and structures. Your child will want to measure many things around the house or yard including people. Children enjoy having a special measuring place to chart their growth such as a closet. Put a mark above the child's head with the date. Mark it on their birthday, or whenever they may ask. They grow very fast in the early years.
- Add something else into your block play such as a toy car to drive along the line of blocks.
- Use an empty laundry basket or box and toss the blocks into the container, counting as you toss. Place a number card beside blocks such as "1" with 1 block, "2" with 2 blocks so that they understand the quantity concept of numbering.
- Hide some blocks around the room play a game of finding them, announcing the shape or color each time one is found.

The possibilities are endless of what can be done with blocks. You don't need to keep buying more and more toys, but explore all the possibilities of what you already have. According to some experts, children enjoy the feel of wood and metal rather than plastic—and wood and metal are more durable. Great buys can be found at garage sales and community thrift stores or let relatives and friends know you are interested in their unused toys. You may want to temporarily swap toys with friends.

Science
There are three modes of learning: Auditory (listening), Visual (show me and I'll understand) and Kinesthetic (touching, feeling, experiencing). Science activities will help you realize which learning style your child benefits from the most and prefers. Children love to explore nature and their world. They are interested in:

- Gravity (tossing, throwing, knocking down, pouring)
- Motion and movement (swinging, bouncing, sliding, running, jumping)
- Things changing in form and texture such as in Jello, ice cubes melting, water beads, shaving cream mixed with food coloring, playdough made with various textures and scents, and participating in cooking and baking.
- Balancing (walking on a beam or a board raised on the ground, tricycles, bicycles, scooter, skates)
- Learning about animals and their life cycles such as the metamorphous of butterflies and mealworms changing into beetles.

Provide a naturally curious child with a few exploration tools such as magnets, a magnifying glass, insect net, bug box. Help them label collections of whatever interests them. Let children get messy with water, dirt, mud puddles, and sand. Let your child spread peanut butter on a pinecone or empty roll, roll in bird seed, and hang it from a tree for their personalized birdfeeder. Teach children to respect the earth through recycling materials, re-using containers, restoring broken toys, and replenishing the earth by planting a garden or tree.

Children love books that teach about our fascinating world such as animals, fish, birds, leaves, flowers, trees, gardening and the weather.

- Read critter books such as Rainbow Fish, The Very Quiet Cricket, The Three Little Pigs, and The Very Busy Spider
- Take a trip to the pet store or zoo
- Visit the children's science or nature section in your local library. Ask the librarian to recommend books or host an activity for preschoolers involving science. Many communities have a "Critter Man" who will bring various creatures for the children to learn about and perhaps touch.

A man who carries a cat by the tail learns something he can learn in no other way. ~ Mark Twain

Chapter Eleven
Summary and Resources

We hope that by now you are already seeing the benefits of playfully challenging your child and hopefully you even have more free time! If you are interested in learning more from us, you can visit us on our blogs and sign up to receive our posts via email. Please feel free to contact us with ideas and questions. If you are new to Pinterest, Katie's blog has information on how to join and how it works.

Blogs

Katie's blog: mommywithselectivememory.blogspot.com
Susan's blog: www.Kindergartenbasics.blogspot.com

Pinterest

Katie's Pinterest Address: www.pinterest.com/HappyMommyHB
Susan's Pinterest Address: www.pinterest.com/susanjcase
Kid Blogger Network:
www.pinterest.com/playdrmom/kid-blogger-network-activities-crafts
created by Laura Hutchinson at blog.playdrhutch.com.
I'm a Kid-Friendly Blog:
www.pinterest.com/handsonaswegrow/i-m-a-kid-friendly-blog
created by Jamie Reimer at www.handsonaswegrow.com

Books

Covey, Stephen R. (1999). *The Seven Habits of Highly Effective Families.*
Crain, William (1999). *Theories of Development.*
Elkind, David (2007). *The Hurried Child.*

Elkind, David (2007). *The Power of Play: Learning What Comes Naturally.*

Fay, Jim and Cline, Foster (2011). *Parenting with Love and Logic: Teaching Children Responsibility.*

Fay, Jim and Fay, Charles (2006). *Love and Logic Magic for Early Childhood: Practical Parenting from Birth to Six Years.*

Hirsh-Pasek, Kathy and Golinkoff, Roberta M. *(2003). Einstein Never Used Flashcards: How Our Children Really Learn—and Why They Need to Play More and Memorize Less.*

Marano, Hara Estroff and Skenazy, Lenore (Spring 2011) *American Journal of Play.* "Why Parents Should Stop Overprotecting Kids and Let Them Play." Volume 3, number 4.

Miller, Karen (2000). *Things to Do With Toddlers and Twos.*

Morgan, Amanda (2010). *Parenting with Positive Guidance: Tools for Building Discipline from the Inside Out.*

Neufeld, Gordon and Mate, Gabor (2008). *Hold On To Your Kids: Why Parents Need to Matter More Than Peers.*

Skenazy, Lenore (2009). *Free-Range Kids: How to Raise Safe, Self-Reliant Children*

Weissbluth, Marc *(2009). Healthy Sleep Habits, Happy Child.*

When in doubt, just take the next small step to help your child playfully learn, because children only have one childhood. And always remember: You are enough.